An Odyssey in Print

An Odyssey in Print

ADVENTURES IN THE SMITHSONIAN LIBRARIES

Mary Augusta Thomas

WITH A FOREWORD BY *Nancy E. Gwinn*

AND ESSAYS BY *Michael Dirda*
AND *Storrs L. Olson*

Smithsonian Institution Press

Washington and London

This book was published on the occasion of the exhibition *Voyages: A Smithsonian Libraries Exhibition,* on view at the Grolier Club, 47 East 60th Street, New York, New York, May 16–August 4, 2001. Under the name *An Odyssey in Print: Adventures in the Smithsonian Libraries,* the same exhibition opens in the Smithsonian Institution Libraries Gallery, located in the National Museum of American History, Behring Center, Constitution Avenue and 14th Street NW, Washington, D.C., May 2002–May 2003.

The exhibition can be seen on-line at www.sil.si.edu/Exhibitions

The exhibition, programs, and publications were made possible by the generous support of UBS Warburg UBS Paine Webber. Additional contributions were made by Credit Suisse First Boston, the Carl and Lily Pforzheimer Foundation, the Gladys Krieble Delmas Foundation, Morgan Stanley, and the 1999–2000 Smithsonian Institution Libraries Board: Rosemary Livingston Ripley (Chair), Jeannine S. Clark, Shirley M. Gifford, Richard E. Gray, Brian J. Heidtke, John B. Henry, Margery F. Masinter, Barbara J. Smith, and Frank A. Weil.

Library of Congress Cataloging-in-Publication Data
Smithsonian Institution. Libraries.
    An odyssey in print : adventures in the Smithsonian Libraries / Mary Augusta Thomas ; with a foreword by Nancy E. Gwinn ; and essays by Michael Dirda and Storrs L. Olson.
      p. cm.
    Catalog of an exhibition held at the Grolier Club, New York, May 16–Aug. 4, 2001, and at the Smithsonian Institution Libraries Gallery, Washington, May 2002–May 2003.
      Includes index.
     ISBN: 1-58834-036-8 (alk. paper)
     1. Smithsonian Institution. Libraries—Exhibitions.
2. Library resources—Washington (D.C.)—Exhibitions.
3. Books—History—Exhibitions. 4. Smithsonian Institution. Libraries. I. Thomas, Mary Augusta. II. Dirda, Michael. III. Olson, Storrs L. IV. Title.
z733.s67 s65 2002
027.573—dc21   2001049736

Endleaves: "Map of the Known World," from Ptolemy, *Liber geographiae* (Book of geography), 1511.

Frontispiece: "Attacked by the Giant Reptile," from Dick Calkins, *Buck Rogers, 25th Century,* ca. 1935.

John Tsantes photographed items in the Smithsonian Libraries collection, with the following exceptions: pages 12, 14, and 144 by Matt Flynn, and pages 7, 9, 10, and 49 by Jon Goell; and pages 21, 24, 26, 44, 48, 52, 54, 63, 78, 80, 86, 105, 113, 119, 129, 131, 139, 143, 148, 149, 167, and 173 by the Office of Imaging, Printing, and Photographic Services, Smithsonian Institution. Images on pages 141 and 154 were digitized by the Smithsonian Libraries Imaging Center. The photographs on pages 6 and 27 were provided by the Smithsonian Institution Archives.

The image of the Sears catalog on page 164 is reprinted by arrangement with Sears, Roebuck and Co. and is protected under copyright. No duplication is permitted.

The image from Charles A. Lindbergh's *We* on page 91, copyright 1927, renewed © 1955 by Charles A. Lindbergh, is used by permission of G. P. Putnam's Sons, division of Penguin Putnam Inc.

Every effort has been made to secure permission to reproduce the images illustrated herein. If omissions are noted, please contact the Smithsonian Institution Libraries, National Museum of Natural History, 10th and Constitution Ave. NW, Washington, D.C. 20560.

For permission to reproduce illustrations appearing in this book, please correspond directly with the owners of the works, as listed in the individual captions, or with the Smithsonian Institution Libraries. The Smithsonian Institution Press does not retain reproduction rights for these illustrations individually or maintain a file of addresses for photo sources.

Edited by Suzanne Kotz
Designed by Susan E. Kelly
Typeset by Jennifer L. Sugden
Produced by Marquand Books, Inc., Seattle
  www.marquand.com
Printed and bound by C&C Offset Printing Co., Ltd., Hong Kong; not at government expense

09 08 07 06 05 04 03 02 5 4 3 2 1

Contents

KONRAD GESNER, *Historia animalium*
(History of animals), 1551–87, with
pigskin binding.

The Smithsonian Institution Libraries

Anacostia Museum & Center for
African American History and Culture Library

Anthropology Library

Botany Library

Central Reference & Loan Services

Cooper-Hewitt, National Design Museum
Library (New York, New York)

The Dibner Library of the History of
Science and Technology

Freer Gallery of Art and
Arthur M. Sackler Gallery Library

Hirshhorn Museum and
Sculpture Garden Library

Horticulture Library

Museum Reference Center

Museum Support Center Library
(Suitland, Maryland)

National Air and Space Museum Library

National Museum of African Art Library

National Museum of American History Library

National Museum of the American Indian Library
(Suitland, Maryland)

National Museum of Natural History Library

National Postal Museum

National Zoological Park Library

Natural History Rare Book Library

Smithsonian American Art Museum /
National Portrait Gallery Library

Smithsonian Environmental Research Center
Library (Edgewater, Maryland)

Smithsonian Tropical Research Institute Library
(Republic of Panama)

The Smithsonian Institution Building, north side, 1865–1900.
Smithsonian Institution Archives (record unit 95, box 30,
neg. 11168).

Foreword

*I*n August 1846 the *New York Evening Post* reported on the activities of the Twenty-ninth Congress: "The most gratifying act of the whole of the session was the unexpected passage of the Smithsonian Institution bill." "Unexpected" was the correct term, since Congress had for ten years debated the nature of the organization that should be created from the equally unexpected bequest of an English geologist, James Smithson—and members had seemed no closer to a decision. For the United States to have the opportunity, at one stroke, to create a national institution that would command the respect of—if not actually rival— the great libraries and scientific institutions of Europe was unforseen, but once the decision was made, the young country rose to the challenge. For was not 1846 the year in which the United States captured its prevailing spirit of expansion and confidence in speaking of its "manifest destiny" to spread to the farthest shore of the continent? And did not the growth of industry, transportation and communication systems, and technological genius seem to make all things seem possible?

As curator Mary Augusta Thomas points out in her historical essay, Congress incorporated a library into the blueprint of the Smithsonian Institution at its origin. The history of library development in the Institution mirrors that of the Smithsonian's

Smithsonian librarian and Smithsonian curator of invertebrate zoology in the Charles Coffin Jewett Room, Arts and Industries Building, where portions of the Libraries' natural history rare book collections are housed. Photo: © 1999 Jon Goell.

155 years of political maneuvering, financial blessings and hardship, curious episodes, and fascinating personalities. What has since remained true and steady, as ornithologist Storrs L. Olson's essay readily acknowledges, is the centrality of the marvelous library collections and their close association with artifacts and specimens, as well as with

the heritage of scientific and humanistic inquiry that forms the foundation of the Smithsonian's contribution to the nation.

And magnificent collections they are! This catalog can only tantalize the reader with a mere trace of the riches that have been acquired over the past century to support the research, exhibition, and education programs of this far-flung enterprise. Recognizing the wealth of library resources in the Washington area, and given our special relationship with the Library of Congress, Smithsonian Libraries staff carefully select each and every title to ensure that it specifically advances the Institution's work. Consequently, the Libraries' collections display extraordinary depth in narrowly defined fields that mirror the current and historical interests of the curatorial and scientific staff. Even so, the range is broad: from African and Asian art to contemporary American art and portraiture and European decorative art and design; from tropical biology, ecology, and molecular systematics to Renaissance science and the history of scientific instrumentation; from American political and business history to technology, aviation, and space flight; from research on endangered species to conservation of religious *santos*. As part of a sixteen-museum community, the Libraries places equal weight on the intellectual content and artifactual significance of its volumes. They are to be both read and exhibited.

An Odyssey in Print: Adventures in the Smithsonian Libraries comes at a singular moment in the history of the Smithsonian Institution Libraries. Secretary S. Dillon Ripley created the Libraries when, in 1968, he consolidated the numerous sprawling and dispersed book collections of the Institution into a centralized system. Its first director, Russell Shank, set about transforming the Libraries into a state-of-the-art operation to provide Smithsonian researchers, scientists, scholars, and students—wherever they might be located—with a strong, consistent complement of information services, resources, and research tools. Shank modernized operations and, for the first time, reached out beyond the Institution to connect the Libraries with the greater professional community. He joined the Association of Research Libraries and the Federal Library Committee and signed on with the Ohio Computer Library Center (OCLC) for computerized cataloging. Shank greatly increased the profile of the Smithsonian when he became the president of the prestigious American Library Association. With one eye on the future, we continue to contribute enthusiastically to the library profession and use our ever-expanding network of relationships to improve services. We have never looked back.

Now the Smithsonian Libraries is in the midst of a second monumental transformation that stimulates us to rise to the challenges and opportunities represented by fast-changing information technology and the new digital world. Moving optimistically into the twenty-first century, we are faced with the task of stretching our budget to support and integrate what seem to be two distinct libraries—the physical and the virtual—to satisfy our users.

Regardless of what many assume about the availability of information on the Internet, most of the world continues to publish substantive work in the traditional way—on paper, bound between covers. Over the past decade, publishers in both the United States and the United Kingdom published each year many more than 100,000 separate titles. The Libraries must continue to acquire an appropriate selection of these and other publications and maintain the cataloging, shelving, binding, and preservation work flows to make

left Stabilizing a rare book. Photo: © 1999 Jon Goell.
right Inspecting a master microfilm negative.
Photo: © 1999 Jon Goell.

them readily accessible. This work is traditional and easily understood, just as the historical methods used by scientists and historians to make use of collections have been. Thus the Libraries catalogs the print collections and preserves them through the efforts of a Book Conservation Laboratory and through such techniques as microfilming, binding, protecting with customized boxes and other acid-free containers, repairing, and ensuring the best environments in all locations where our collections are housed.

The world is changing, however. The ubiquity of the Internet, combined with inexpensive computers containing huge storage capacities, is inexorably broadening the skills and tools required to obtain information and accomplish work. To accommodate this change, library collections must be dynamic and continue to take in the result of human intellectual enterprise in whatever forms it comes. Electronic books and journals, new databases, digital-only publications, listservs and chat rooms—and of course email—are now standard ingredients of the twenty-first-century library. Handling the digital side of the library at a minimum stretches traditional work flows. In fact, it

often requires a wholly separate set of routines and operations based on practices that not only are not standardized but also are in a continuing process of invention. Negotiating licenses substitutes for purchasing subscriptions. Buying access substitutes for buying books. Digital editions substitute for paper and microfilm. Computer disks and hard drives substitute for photocopies. Metadata substitutes for cataloging. Email substitutes for the telephone.

It is an exhilarating time for librarians, because our traditional skills of organizing knowledge into meaningful categories have been thrown into high relief by the digital age. The new mission statement of the Smithsonian Libraries reflects the blend of

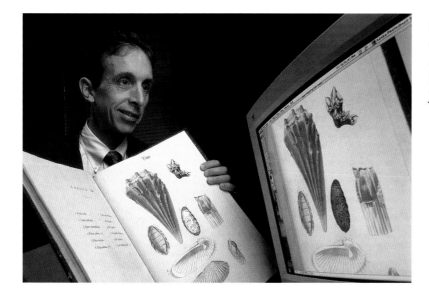

Digitizing J. J. N. A. Spalowsky's 1801 edition of *Prodromus in systema historiam testaceorum* in the Smithsonian Institution Libraries Imaging Center. Photo: © 1999 Jon Goell.

our two worlds as well as our new status and the services we are called on to perform:

We will be catalyst, partner, and participant in the use of information technology and the transformation of scholarly research in the sciences, arts, and cultural heritage of the United States.

We shall preserve and organize our collections and shall use the most appropriate and innovative means to enrich and augment them.

It is also an exhilarating time for the Smithsonian as the Institution seeks aggressively to broaden its public outreach, share its collections widely, and integrate itself more firmly in the minds and hearts of the American public. The Libraries embraces a new, energetic role in serving the general public, made possible by the Internet. The Libraries traditionally has always shared its collections and information expertise outside the Smithsonian. In 2000, for example, we answered 97,000 information queries, half of which came from outside the Institution, and sent through interlibrary loan more than 10,000

books and articles to library users in all fifty states and fourteen countries. We watched "hits" to our website leap to well over one million per month. Whether the request is for information on butterfly plants or snow leopards, for names of carpet manufacturing firms or Rajasthani painting, for Pueblo architecture or the color of the bombs carried by the Boeing B-17 in World War II, our reference librarians are ready to assist.

We shall provide vigorous, responsive service to meet the needs of an increasingly diverse institutional and public clientele.

Now, through the Internet, we can serve more people with resources that help them answer their own questions. To do this, we have begun to transform ourselves by creating new facilities and by training staff for positions that did not exist five years ago. In 1999 the Libraries opened its new digital Imaging Center whose work is overseen by a Digital Imaging Specialist. A Digital Library Coordinator has designed our new website, the Smithsonian Libraries Galaxy of Knowledge (www.sil.si.edu), which contains full texts of rare and special books and other materials with full-color illustrations, special indexes, and other features. Online exhibitions at this site place library materials in thematic displays ranging from the building of the Panama Canal to the life of Edward S. Curtis, famous photographer of Native Americans, to the history and technology of laying under-ocean cables that link continents. The Galaxy contains specialized guides to subjects in which our collections are strong. It is for information seekers in school and information seekers in life.

We shall interpret our collections for the general public, using them as the basis for exhibitions, publications, and public programs that advance an understanding of scientific and technological progress, the arts, and the American experience.

The transformation to the twenty-first-century library is far from complete. Perhaps it never will be. After all, the process of modernization in today's world means constant and continual change. There is a certainty, however. While to exist, a library must have collections, to live, it must have people—an excellent staff and supporters who value our intellectual and cultural heritage and are committed to its survival. Our mission underscores our commitment to staff.

We shall foster in our staff common goals of excellence, innovation, and cooperation and ensure that all are highly trained, technologically sophisticated, and thoroughly committed to the Smithsonian's research, education, and public outreach mandate.

Our supporters recognize that change requires investment far beyond the Smithsonian's normal operating budget. That is why in 1997 the Institution's Board of Regents created a board of citizens from around the country to advise, promote, and raise funds for the extraordinary needs of the

Libraries. Their contributions, along with those of the Gladys Krieble Delmas Foundation, made this catalog possible. Two years later, the Libraries launched the Spencer Baird Society, its premier donor recognition organization, which provides unrestricted funds for such purposes as the Baird Society Resident Scholar Program. We value our donors highly and provide events and activities that engage them in the Smithsonian's work and programs, an association that helps to solidify our public purpose. We invite to join us all who would enjoy a fruitful relationship with the Smithsonian Institution through its Libraries.

So now sit back, read with pleasure the outstanding essays by Michael Dirda, Mary Augusta Thomas, and Storrs L. Olson, and explore the tempting hints of the treasures to be found in the Smithsonian Institution Libraries. We hope it will stimulate you to make a real journey to Washington, D.C., and a virtual journey to our website to sample more of the splendors to be found. They are journeys you will surely enjoy.

Nancy E. Gwinn
Director
Smithsonian Institution Libraries

Percy black & puts him down in white, with a bold hand:

Aa Bb Cc Dd Ee Ff Gg Hh Ii Jj Kk Ll Mm Nn Oo Pp Qq Rr Ss Tt Uu Vv Ww Xx Yy Z

Walter Crane, *A Romance of the Three Rs,* 1886.

Realms of Wonder / Michael Dirda

In Balzac's first great novel, *La peau de chagrin* (The fatal skin), a desperate young man, caught up in the suicidal despair common to romantic heroes, wanders into a curious secondhand shop. As Raphael de Valentin penetrates deeper and deeper into the store's crowded interior, Balzac evokes a realm of almost unimaginable richness: strange relics, Oriental treasures, the alluring artifacts of faraway civilizations. Think of Aladdin's cave, as imagined by Disney. So dazzling, in fact, is the sheer abundance, the uncanny plenitude, that Raphael nearly swoons from vertigo; there seems no end to this heaped-up, jumbled splendor.

For Americans the closest equivalent to this spooky emporium is the Smithsonian Institution. We expect "America's attic" to contain marvels, unique specimens, everything and anything. Don't we half suspect that deep in its vaults one will almost certainly find the Ark of the Covenant, a working Time Machine, the Holy Grail, the Missing Link, and the sword Excalibur? After all, doesn't Indiana Jones do the Institution's fieldwork? Isn't Merlin, ill-disguised in suit and repp tie, one of the curators?

This, I think, is how most of us imagine— would like to imagine—the Smithsonian museums. But fewer of us realize that this vast theater of wonders also includes a library. Or rather a collection of libraries. Yet this exhibition, *An Odyssey in Print: Adventures in the Smithsonian Libraries,* reminds us that the same scholars who collected flora and fauna also gathered together folios. Just consider: the hundred or so rare items on display include an early printing of Pliny's natural history; a volume of Ptolemy's maps of the ancient world; Konrad Gesner's Renaissance encyclopedia of animals; Captain Cook's account of his voyages around the world; Mark Catesby's eighteenth-century natural history; a rare early edition of Linnaeus's *Systema naturae,* which established the two-part method for naming the world's species; *Walden,* inscribed by Thoreau; the original published account of the Montgolfier brothers' balloon ascension; and a copy of *First on the Moon,* signed by the astronauts Neil Armstrong, Edwin Aldrin, and Michael Collins. And more. Much more. This superb exhibition honors a great library, one which not only preserves treasures of the past

but also makes them available to scholars as research tools for the present. The books presented in *An Odyssey in Print* possess the same range and importance as any of the celebrated artworks and artifacts of the Smithsonian's museums.

All these volumes—even the ones in Latin, perhaps particularly the ones in Latin—offer us more than pages of history or examples of how people once understood and guessed at the nature of the world around, above, or below them. They are, in truth, spell-books. Their ink, images, and leather bindings, even their metal clasps, possess a halo, a nimbus of the magical and unique. We peer at these pages as into a scryer's glass—and find worlds within the words. Here Europe confronts the peoples of the Pacific for the first time, in a moment that will never come again. Here the sea charts may still blazon forth "Beyond this point be dragons," and *mappamundi* designate the vast realm of the Christian sorcerer-king, the elusive Prester John. Stare hard at the old woodcuts and you will discern unicorns in the garden, hippogriffs and manticores romping with giraffes and alligators.

Indeed, here is all the lost world of mankind's childhood. Such volumes are the "nonfiction" equivalent of those "stories wanderers told in hall when the world was young"—and, as Clark B. Firestone reminds us in *The Coasts of Illusion*, "in out-of-the-way places still they tell them, and men believe." Paradoxically, though, from these ostensibly outmoded views of nature, we absorb a reinvigorated sense of the Earth's ceaseless, glorious richness. They remind us that there was once a time when at least some things were new under the sun.

Old books, in particular, have always seemed vessels of power, with a kind of holy mana emanating from their decorated pages. In numerous English ghost stories, a well-meaning, if slightly hapless, antiquary will unearth a locked box or calculate the existence of a secret chamber in an old church wall. Therein he will almost always discover an ancient manuscript or codex. And just as we know that the pretty girl in slasher movies should never open the heavy door to the basement, so we realize—as donnish Reverend Maitland or Professor Trueheart reaches out to touch the disconcertingly bright vellum binding, adorned with hieroglyphs—that there must have been a very good reason to imprison this volume, and that all hell, or at least a hungry, ravening spirit, is probably about to break loose. Because invariably that seeming treasure turns out to be some nefarious sorcerer's grimoire, or even the dread *Necronomicon* of the infamous wizard Abdul Alhazred. (For details, see respectively the ghostly tales of M. R. James and the horror stories of H. P. Lovecraft.)

Today the omnipresence of paperbacks and the easy availability of most common titles, as well as the flashy glamour of the Internet, may occasionally dispel some of the mystery surrounding books—at least for adults, if not for young Harry Potter fans. Hurrying through our workdays and our grown-up lives, we tend to regard books as containers of text first, forgetful that they are also objects, examples of physical beauty, sources of delight, almost toys. Try, though, to remember your first visit to the public library as a child: row after serried row of picture books and young adult novels, colorful, enticing, magical . . . and free for the taking (so long as you had a library card). Even now watch a six-year-old studying the picture albums in a children's reading room. See how she weighs a book's worth by its title or cover illustration, perhaps pauses to murmur aloud its opening sentence, then thoughtfully places *Jumanji* or *Dinosaur Bob* or *The Big Orange Splot* on the pile of the chosen for check-out that week. I will never forget the sheer astonishment I felt as a boy when a kindly librarian informed me that I could take home as many books as I could carry. It was like being told one could pocket all the penny candy in the jar, buy all the Barbies or G.I. Joes in the toy store.

Look with a child's eyes at these treasures of the Smithsonian Libraries, and you may still feel a bit

of that preadolescent enchantment. Here is a little book, in German, describing the pleasures of traveling across the ocean by zeppelin. Here is sheet music, from early in the century, about journeying to the moon. Not least, here is an interleaved biography of the Wright brothers, in which an ardent collector has managed, astonishingly, to inveigle signatures from virtually every major figure in the history of American aviation, including not only Charles Lindbergh but also Dwight D. Eisenhower.

Just as early books, no matter how theological their content, contain a whiff of sulfur and the Mephistophelean, so time gives to more recent paper ephemera a patina of lost innocence. Imagine: In one picture—from that piece of sheet music—sophisticated Jazz Agers stroll along the veranda of their snazzy rocket, flirting and sipping highballs, as they wend their way through space. It's almost a twentieth-century version of Watteau's tableau of eighteenth-century couples, boarding a ship that will take them to Cythera, the misty island of love. We glance at these laughing people and smile at the romantic shortsightedness—no problems with air, gravity, cosmic detritus—but don't we also envy this earlier era, when the world seemed a happier place? After all, Norman Rockwell remains our national painter, and one of the most popular books of recent years is Jack Finney's *Time and Again,* in which a modern man escapes back to late-nineteenth-century New York—and to a better life. As Keats famously observed, books are "charmed magic casements, opening on the foam / Of perilous seas in faery lands forlorn"— or on Gibson girls and dashing spies out of E. Phillips Oppenheim.

In another poem, Tennyson's "Ulysses," the Greek hero—and pagan saint for all voyages of discovery—finds that he has grown restless on

Ithaca and craves the excitement of the ocean and its dangers. Most of the items in this show disclose a similar kind of restlessness in their authors: these are scholar-adventurers, sailing on strange seas of thought, mapping unexplored realms, testing the currents, boldly going where no one has gone before. New discoveries, earth-shaking ideas, faraway places, exotic creatures—all these can be found in these wonderful highlights from the Smithsonian Libraries.

Still, there is another kind of yearning, not for the new, but for the Great Good Place, a snug hobbit-hole, a private refuge. Isn't this what collectors try to create? To fabricate, out of books and objects, a world more suited to our personalities than that noisy, unhappy one outside our windows? To satisfy a little of that unassuageable human longing for something more out of life than what our era allows us? I know a Sherlock Holmes fan who has tried to reproduce the great detective's digs at 221-B Baker Street. I've visited a government bureaucrat who has turned his apartment into a homage to the Jazz Age, with posters of the Twentieth-Century Limited barreling toward infinity, a stand-up radio and Art Deco furniture, a bookcase of best-sellers of the 1920s and 1930s. I've met a businessman who built an addition to his house as a shrine to P. G. Wodehouse, outfitting it with first editions and memorabilia honoring the creator of Jeeves, Bertie Wooster, and Blandings Castle. And I've known more than a few science fiction fans who have preserved the gosh-wow wonder of the early pulps in basements or rec rooms chockablock with framed issues of *Astounding*, replicas of Tom Corbett ray guns, and models of Bug-Eyed Monsters.

To those unhappily immune to the collecting urge, my friends probably seem like eccentrics, nuts, geeky nerds. But in fact they remind us of a great, if often disparaged, truth: things can make us happy. We decorate our houses and offices to re-create, in miniature, the conditions of paradise as we imagine them. As a college student, I once spent an evening at the home of a distinguished professor of history, by then retired. The woodwork in his rambling old Victorian house was dark, the halls wide, floors covered with Oriental rugs; framed prints by Piranesi hung on the wall. The library was dominated by a huge antique globe and a refectory table, with two green-domed study lamps. The books on his floor-to-ceiling shelves were all in hardcover, most of them old, their spines bare of gaudy and distracting dust jackets. Remember Henry Higgins's study/laboratory in *My Fair Lady*? It was something like that. And I instantly knew that this house, this room, was my lost Eden. And I've longed, in vain, to duplicate it ever since.

And that, of course, is one reason why museums and libraries are invaluable. Yes, they preserve the legacy of our past, and, yes, the knowledge they hold can be practical or Utopian, or even an end in itself. But a place like the Smithsonian is, in a way, also a branch of our own private collection, the off-site vault where we store our truly rare treasures. If an American needs to see a Catesby or Audubon or Pliny, he knows where they can be found. We can come and, with the proper credentials, turn their pages, marvel, refresh our spirits, check our facts, study the illustrations. So, too, with library exhibitions. Not only do they give immediate pleasure through their beauty or oddity, they also remind us that certain books *exist,* that they are part of our heritage. Simply to peruse such treasures makes one feel a little wiser, more civilized, almost learned.

Of course, collecting can easily spin out of control, and what may start out as a collection may grow wildly into an accumulation and finally end up a mere heap. One local bookman's house grew so clotted with his acquisitions that he simply tossed new purchases down into the basement, slowly engrossing that subterranean space with mildewing print. And all collectors, inevitably, recall the story of the Collyer brothers, one of whom was crushed by mounds of newspapers, leaving the other, disabled and unable to get out for provisions, to suffer a grisly death by starvation.

No, a true collection obviously requires organization, else nothing can be located and chaos is come again. In fact, many of the books represented in this marvel-filled show focus on the desire to discover (or impose) an order on the world's variety and the Earth's overwhelming fecundity. Maps guide us through unseen geographies. Scientific nomenclature orders Nature herself, making clear the connections between species. Volumes of natural history organize thousands of animals and plants. Meanwhile, as logbooks chart the progress of explorations, so cosmographies make sense of the starry heavens and laboratory journals describe the microscopic wonders found in a drop of muddy pond water.

Order and surprise: these are two intertwined elements that make for any great library or collection. Consider the pleasure, and virtue, of each.

A collector of, say, all the books published by the firm of Covici-Friede drives off on a Saturday morning, visiting yard sales, thrift stores, Value Villages, specialty shops. He spends his free time scanning book dealer's catalogs; at lunch he browses the Net's secondhand sites. From this jungle of material he may pluck out one or two titles, which he adds to his Covici-Friede holdings at home. Meanwhile, other collectors are covering the same ground, tracking Regency romances, locked-room mysteries, novels written by poets, volumes with the word "doctor" or "dawn" in the

PROJECTILE TRAINS FOR THE MOON.

Frontispiece.   [p. 95.]

Frontispiece in JULES VERNE, *From the Earth to the Moon . . . ,* 1874.

Willy Ley, *Die Möglichkeit der Weltraumfahrt*
(The feasibility of interplanetary travel), 1928.

title, what have you. In essence, this restless activity transforms the tropical rain forest of titles, overgrown with lianas and chokeweed, into those graceful, well-hedged gardens in which it is a pleasure to wander on a summer's evening. How deeply gratifying it can be just to scan a bookcase arrayed with travelers' memoirs and reminiscences about, say, the search for the headwaters of the Nile, or entirely devoted to the art of papermaking, or to works by and about William Faulkner or John Dickson Carr or Georgette Heyer. A distinguished bibliographer of my acquaintance owns several hundred editions of John Bunyan's *Pilgrim's Progress,* and by surveying his shelves, he can grasp

three-and-a-half centuries of human history. The critic Cyril Connolly once likened the feeling of standing before his own collection of modern firsts to that of a captain at the helm of his clipper ship. Any bibliophile will recognize that sense of confidence, calm, well-being, and pleasure.

Great public libraries, like that of the Smithsonian, raise this same classifying process to an even higher level. The main collections gather vast quantities of material, imposing the established ordering systems of Dewey or the Library of Congress. But thematic shows, such as this one, can create other special, unexpected arrangements, and these are intended to surprise us. *Voyages* presents titles that are either literally or metaphorically about journeys, and so the discoveries of Galileo butt up against Jolly Jump-Up pop-up books. As a result, for the attentive visitor, the exhibition itself becomes a voyage of discovery: "Oh, I never thought to find this here" or "Who would have expected that title?" All these shocks of recognition actually arise from bringing the ordinarily disparate suddenly together. Yet what is knowledge, after all, but the ability to make such connections? What, too, is connoisseurship, on whatever level of sophistication, but the pleasure of seeing those connections?

A great museum always surprises by its acquisitions. Each of us is bound in time, and we can seldom guess which aspects of our culture will prove valuable to the future. First editions of *The Maltese Falcon* are hard to find in untattered dust jackets at least in part because Hammett's novel was just a mystery, hardly worth bothering about, except as a good weekend read. Now it's worth $25,000. In my own youth, I collected comic books, eventually amassing several hundred—all of which my mother, in the way of mothers through eternity, gave away when I left home. They were, after all, just old funny books to her, hardly worth thinking twice about. Except that now, those first fifty issues of *Green Lantern* and some of the other choicer items would make a tidy down payment on a retirement condo for Mom. If, of course, I still had them.

Unlike spring-cleaning mothers, our museums, libraries, and serious collectors gather up, rather than discard, the disdained and rejected productions of our culture, knowing that one day it will be impossible to find the ephemeral throwaway, the obscure journal, the ball-game scorecard, and relatively easy to locate what everyone recognized as obviously "important." Clearly, as a nation, we need places like the Smithsonian, in its collective wisdom preserving what the rest of us cast off, keeping safe the strange oddments that have come its way, carefully cataloging, ordering, and storing artifacts, specimens, all sorts of printed matter. When, in some unimaginable future, we decide we need this or that book, such institutions will raise our tomes from the tombs.

There is something reassuring about such a venture—and soothing about libraries in general. What reader hasn't occasionally fantasized about a quiet life as a small-town librarian in one of those picture-postcard New England villages? Stroll to work under majestic chestnut trees. Spend the day amid dark mahogany tables and beautifully arranged bookshelves. Tell ghost stories and tall tales during Saturday children's hour. Help middle schoolers research term papers on Lavoisier, the industrial products of Portugal, the history of aluminum. Maybe even smile at the old geezers asleep behind newspapers in the periodicals room. And serenely listen to the susurration of soft voices, the giggles of teenaged girls, whispering about the boys at the next table. A rewarding quiet existence, in need of a Thomas Gray to write its elegy.

After all, visiting an exhibition like *Voyages* leads one, for a moment, away from the hubbub and heartaches of the daily whir, so that we begin to think about other more serious matters. What do we really want from life? Instead of the usual dream of riches, power, and celebrity, a collection of books like these subtly imparts a wish to better ourselves, to try things not yet attempted, to practice a kind of noble ambition, something worthy of Kepler or Darwin, above all, to live a life of consequence. Many of the volumes in this show testify to such admirable obsession in their authors, some of whom carried on in the face of deepening self-doubt, public vilification, or even the threat of death. Thoreau said that he went to the woods "to live deliberately, to front only the essential facts of life," so that when he came to die, he would not "discover that I had not lived." The mere presence of great books can make one eager to measure up to them. As Bertrand Russell once said, they "rouse and stimulate the love of mental adventure."

Mental adventure . . . isn't that the very definition of reading? Even though *Voyages* emphasizes books as historical artifacts or curiosities, just being among so many deeply fascinating titles quite naturally fosters a desire to read and learn. You can't take a six-year-old to a toy store without her wanting to buy something—the mere presence of such ludic plenty sets a child's want-hormones on overdrive.

And yet, as Sartre asked long ago in *What Is Literature?*, why bother to read at all? Tom Clancy, author of *The Hunt for Red October* and numerous other thrillers, gave one of the most succinct answers to this question: "The only way to do all the things you'd like to do is read." We are, alas, linear beings in a hypertext world, and we only get to play the great game once: that's the real tragedy of life.

Robert Frost observed that "two roads diverged in a yellow wood," and he was sorry that he couldn't travel both. In fact, the world is chockablock with intersections, and there are myriad roads we'd like to go down . . . and can't. If you want to become the greatest swordsman in all France or the best bond attorney in New York or tend a bar in Key West, you probably won't also become a Mississippi riverboat gambler, a Buddhist monk, or the finest soprano since Callas. Life is made of choices. Yet people are made of yearnings. Still, through books everything becomes possible. Reading allows us to escape from the seemingly inflexible boundaries of our personal selves. Books don't just open up the world to us, they open us up, too. Kafka claimed, in a violent image, that "a book should be an ax for the frozen sea within us."

Except for love and the making of art, there is in fact no deeper pleasure than one's involvement with a book. "The true use," wrote Harold Bloom in *The Western Canon*, "of Shakespeare or of Cervantes, of Homer or of Dante, of Chaucer or of Rabelais, is to augment one's own growing inner self. Reading deeply in the canon will not make one a better or a worse person, a more useful or more harmful citizen. The mind's dialogue with itself is not primarily a social reality. All that the Western canon can bring one is the proper use of one's solitude, that solitude whose final form is one's confrontation with one's own mortality."

But even in that solitude, books must be read with passion or they are hardly worth reading at all. The boy or girl who eagerly devours *Mad* magazines, *X-Men* comics, and the statistics on the backs of baseball cards may come to love books. All those kids compelled to read—whether the terminally bored or the goody-goody A student who dutifully follows the official curriculum—will probably grow up to regard viewing public television as the absolute acme of cultural achievement. This is in part because too many adults feel they have done their part for literacy by turning the pages of picture books with their toddlers at bedtime—after spending most of the evening slumped in front of televisions or computers. If you want your children to be readers, you must be a reader yourself. Do your kids see you sit down after dinner with a newspaper or novel? Do you frequently say, "Just a minute, I want to finish this chapter"? Is your house filled with books? Not law books or medical manuals, but works of history, fiction, poetry, philosophy? Do you and your family go to the library together? The bookstore? Do you practice the advice of poet Randall Jarrell and "read at whim"?

Most important, do you read aloud with your loved ones? "Reading aloud," wrote children's novelist Joan Aiken of this invaluable practice, "was a daily habit in our family. My mother read aloud to me; she also read to my brother (twelve years older) and to my sister (seven years older). My brother read aloud to my sister; she read aloud to me. My stepfather and my mother read to each other; evening by evening they worked through *War and Peace* or the *Journals* of André Gide, or all the Barchester novels. And I, as soon as I was old enough to do so, read aloud to anyone who would listen; my mother and I plugged our way steadily through the Bible, one of us reading and the other slicing beans (or whatever); besides this, all of us would sometimes have Reading Tea; every member of the family was allowed to bring a book to the table and silently munch while turning the pages."

My own mother taught me to read some forty-five years ago, while I curled up in her lap, on the floor next to the heat register in our dining room. As she oohed and aahed about pictures of fluffy bunnies and little puppies, my four-year-old self

Signed letter from Galileo to French astronomer Nicolas Peirsec, May 12, 1635.

soon realized that these oblong pages gave my beloved mother a lot of pleasure. It was the inspiration a child needs. Even now what is better than to open a new book tentatively, with indifference even, and to find oneself yet again in thrall—to a writer's prose, to a thriller's plot, to a thinker's mind? Isn't that the true pleasure of the text? The reader's particular bliss? Let the whole wide world crumble, so long as I can read another page. And then another after that. And then a hundred more.

Such, such are the joys of a reader and his book, whether it be bound in leather or limp vellum or book cloth or stiff cardboard. But what, you may wonder, about digitized texts and facsimiles? This is, after all, the twenty-first century, with its science fictional promises of e-books, print-on-demand, and other biblio-marvels. Certainly, works of literature should be made available via the Internet or on CD-ROM: The entire history of the book is that of the ever-increasing availability of any and all texts. In some cases, a searchable CD-ROM provides an invaluable tool for scholars, especially in the case of difficult classics or those without an established definitive version (think of *Piers Plowman*). One can discover all sorts of unexpected linkages, detect unsuspected patterns, make fruitful voyages of discovery. That said, an original, whether a manuscript or a first printing, possesses qualities that will never quite transfer to "pixellated" form.

Consider the item in *An Odyssey in Print* with the romantic title *Sidereus nuncius magna* (The great starry messenger). Shortly after the invention of the telescope, Galileo in 1609 constructed one of these lensed marvels for himself and turned his gaze to the heavens. The very next year, he published this brief account of his discoveries, the first work of modern observational astronomy. In it, Galileo describes his revolutionary sightings of craters on the Moon, individual stars in the Milky Way, the four largest moons of Jupiter. Here, then, is the book that set off a tremor of events that shook the foundation of European thought—and launched an intellectual voyage that would take humankind deeper into the universe. Take a look, too, at the Smithsonian's copy of Newton's *Opticks, or, A Treatise of the Reflections, Refractions, Inflections and Colours of Light*. After Newton presented his concepts about the behavior and characteristics of light, particularly that white light is composed of a spectrum of colors, he formulated a number of questions intended to stimulate further research; these "Queries" were considered the most provocative part of the book. In this 1718 revision of his 1704 work, Newton extended his original sixteen queries to thirty-one. The Smithsonian's copy of this epoch-making volume was owned, and heavily annotated, by Robert Smith (1689–1768), Plumian Professor of Astronomy at Cambridge University and author of the most influential textbook on optics in the eighteenth century.

Such books as these two possess an aura, the sort of uniqueness that Walter Benjamin wrote about in his classic essay, "The Work of Art in the Age of Mechanical Reproduction." Still, in my lifetime, the once obvious sovereignty of books has been shaken by the more popular appeal of, successively, movies, television, videos, and most recently, com-

puters and digital technology. For many young people, printed matter has begun to lose its glamour; intellectual and cultural excitement lies elsewhere. I do suspect that within a hundred years books as we know them will have become collectibles, museum pieces, icons.

It's hardly worth bewailing such developments: people will always need and want art and literature, no matter what the container. My real disquiet lies elsewhere—in the attendant psychology fostered by the Internet and other contemporary media. I sometimes sense that focused reading, the valuing of the kind of scholarship achieved only through years spent in libraries, may be in danger of vanishing from our culture. We now absorb information, often in bits and pieces and sound bites, but the slow, steady interaction with a book while sitting quietly in a chair, the passion for story that good novels generate in a reader, what has been called the pleasure of the text—these acts of attention seem increasingly, to use a pop phrase, "at risk." Books, I. A. Richards claimed, are machines to think with. But now we have the machines themselves to do that "thinking." So where does that leave the books? Where indeed?

I don't have those answers and don't think anyone does. Here, it would seem, lies the next voyage of discovery. Who can now imagine what sorts of items will be in a Smithsonian Libraries exhibition a hundred years from now?

Still, some things aren't likely ever to change. Libraries will always be realms of fantasy, ordered warehouses, storerooms of intellectual provision, bazaars of the bizarre and the forgotten. They remind us that even now, no matter how sexy or strange we may find computers and their associated apparatus, we will always need to read and understand words. Language, arranged to order and surprise—isn't that, in the end, what a book offers us? And everything, wrote the poet Mallarmé a hundred years ago, exists to end up in a book.

Including this wonderful show of some of the treasures in the libraries of the Smithsonian Institution.

Michael Dirda is a writer and editor for the Washington Post Book World. *He received the 1993 Pulitzer Prize for criticism and is the author, most recently, of* Readings: Essays and Literary Entertainments *(2000).*

Smithsonian Institution library accession book, ca. 1858 to ca. 1875, with entries by Jane Turner, "who had for many years performed the duties of librarian with the greatest diligence and faithfulness" (Smithsonian Institution Annual Report, 1888).

A Voyage through the Smithsonian Libraries / Mary Augusta Thomas

"For the Increase and Diffusion of Knowledge..."
(Bequest of James Smithson, 1826)

Building a library is a voyage of discovery. The librarian, by locating books and then organizing them into useful collections, follows the path of any traveler who sets off into the unknown. An explorer navigates new territory, arrives at a destination, and usually names or identifies it. After describing the new place, and creating maps and directions for those who will follow, the traveler returns home to tell others about his or her discoveries. Such reports inspire other explorers to go forward on new journeys. So, too, the librarian embarks on a journey, one that begins with a question. He or she searches catalogs, shelves, and sources to locate what is needed, often gathering critical materials together and describing the search process for others to follow. These reports in turn foster new research that spawns further questions and inquiries.

No one may ever know why an English gentleman-scientist, James Smithson, in 1826 willed his estate first to his nephew and then to the United States, which he had never visited, for the express purpose of founding an institution dedicated to the "increase and diffusion of knowledge." Born in France in 1765, James Lewis Macie (the Duke of Northumberland's illegitimate son, he took his father's family name, Smithson, in 1802) went to England for his education, returned to live in France, and moved finally to Italy, where he died in 1829. Six years later, when his nephew died, solicitors notified the chargé d'affaires for the United States in London of the bequest. He in turn notified Martin Van Buren, then secretary of state, who forwarded the news to President Andrew Jackson. Congress debated accepting foreign—more particularly, English—money but decided to send envoy Richard Rush to London to pursue the probate. In August 1838 Rush returned to Washington, D.C., with eleven boxes containing 105 sacks of gold sovereigns worth $508,318.46, an amount equal to one-sixtieth of the entire federal budget. The boxes also contained Smithson's mineral specimens, several hundred books, and other personal belongings. In 1904 Alexander Graham Bell escorted James Smithson's remains to America for interment in the center of the institution his bequest had created.

Joseph Henry (1797–1878) by Walter Ingalls, about 1872. Smithsonian American Art Museum, gift of Walter Ingalls.

Congress debated the disposition of the bequest for nearly ten years, during which time, as other Smithson beneficiaries died, its value increased to approximately $550,000. Senator Rufus Choate of Massachusetts and his supporters strongly championed using the money for a national library covering all branches of inquiry. Others, including Robert Dale Owens, a social reformer and member of the House of Representatives from New Harmony, Indiana, wanted to heighten support for education and public learning. Debates in the Senate generally supported a European ideal of learning as an end in itself and as a sign of maturing national pride, while the House focused on the practical benefits of the bequest to training in agriculture and industry. Congress finally agreed on a

compromise, which President James K. Polk signed as the Act of Organization on August 10, 1846.

The act transferred most decisions about organization to a new Smithsonian Board of Regents, whose members included the vice president of the United States, the chief justice of the Supreme Court, members of the House and Senate, and citizens. The act did specify construction of a building to contain a library, a museum, lecture halls, and an institute for science, to be operated under the direction of the Secretary of the Smithsonian.

The majority of Strangers who visit the city consider it a very beautiful edifice.
(Smithsonian Institution Annual Report, 1856)

A monstrous pile of misshapen towers, arches, columns . . .
(Dorothea Dix, social reformer, 1852)

Joseph Henry, a scientist, teacher, and scientific entrepreneur, became the first Secretary. His immediate charge was to use the interest that had accumulated—$250,000—since the bequest had been deposited in the U.S. Treasury to construct a building on the flat area below the Capitol. The marshy area was the last place that an educated gentleman or lady would have gone for study. The Smithsonian Building Committee worked closely with noted architect James Renwick Jr. to create a structure that addressed all the activities mandated in the Act of Organization. Renwick looked to history for a model, since a building that housed the multiple functions of library, museum, and scientific research facility did not exist in the United States in 1846. The first book purchased for the Smithsonian library was, not surprisingly, *A Glossary of Terms Used in Grecian, Roman, Italian, and Gothic Architecture,* by John Henry Parker (2nd ed., London, 1838). The work

The Smithsonian's Arts and Industries
Building, exterior, front, north side.
Smithsonian Institution Archives
(record unit 95, box 32, neg. 5787).

supplied Renwick and the Regents with ideas
for the Norman-style design of the Smithsonian
Institution Building, popularly known as the
Castle, which was completed in 1855.

> *Henry . . . designed the Institution to be the cavalry
> of science, free to dart from front to front, giving just
> enough encouragement at one place to insure effective
> work, and able at will, to dash off to another spot
> when the emergency arose.*
> (Charles Greeley Abbot, Proceedings of the Conference
> on the Future of the Smithsonian Institution,
> February 11, 1927)

The Regents' choice of Joseph Henry as the first
Secretary defined the new institution. Henry, of
Princeton University, was the best-known scientist
of his day in America and one of the few also recognized abroad. Because the organizing act failed
to define the exact nature of the Smithsonian, it
fell to Henry to set the purpose of the new academy. He clearly saw a role for the Smithsonian in
developing American science, and his determina-
tion to make the Institution a center for scientific
achievement dominated its early history. Henry
believed that science and its publication was an

"increase" of knowledge, while lectures, schooling, and popular publications would care for "diffusion." Although Henry devoted energy to the required lectures and public programs of the improving sort, his dedication to developing science came first. To encourage new scientific exploration and discovery, Henry gathered the right men to carry out and publish their research under the Smithsonian aegis. The first Smithsonian building included a laboratory or apparatus room, outfitted for explaining science to students and visitors, plus living quarters for Henry, his family, and a few researchers.

Science in the United States at the time was a motley blend of specialties, and its support and publication was disorganized and decentralized at best. Scientific societies began in the colonies in the 1740s with the founding of Philadelphia's American Philosophical Society, followed by the American Academy of Arts and Sciences in Boston in 1780. In Washington, the National Institute, officially founded in 1840 by Joel Poinsett as the National Institution for the Promotion of Science, held the objects gathered during the United States Exploring Expedition of 1838–42, led by Lt. Charles Wilkes. The expedition's findings represented the first organized government survey of the territory of the Pacific Coast, and Poinsett had sought the Smithson bequest to continue the work of the National Institute. Basic science of the sort undertaken in Europe was rare. The new country was forging a more practical scientific identity aimed at improving American agriculture, mining, and industry, and, like other nations, the United States had began surveying its territories for the raw materials coming into demand with the growth of manufacturing. A secondary motive driving the development of American science lay in the mind-set formed by American schools, which stressed pragmatic achievement over the perceived elitism of European academies.

We have embarked together on a perilous voyage and unless the ship is managed with caution and the officers are of the same mind and determined to pull together, we shall be in danger of shipwreck.
(Joseph Henry to Charles Coffin Jewett, March 23, 1847)

While Henry was pursuing his vision of science, Charles Coffin Jewett, librarian at Brown University, was developing his ideas for the American public library. The Act of Organization provided for assistants to the Secretary, and in 1847, at the urging of Senator Choate, Henry appointed Jewett, already a leader in the library profession, to the post of Assistant Secretary, in charge of the library. Henry, in correspondence with his new assistant, manifested his tight managerial style and stressed his vision of the Smithsonian as an agency devoted to scientific research and publication. Encouraged by those Regents who supported a grander plan for a national library, however, Jewett used his Smithsonian position for the benefit and development of libraries across the country.

In 1851 Jewett conducted the first survey of public libraries, which gave an organized description of library service in the United States. Most libraries, he found, were small and lacked even basic scholarly reference works. Jewett and Henry realized that any serious scholar would have to travel miles to many different library collections to complete comprehensive research. Furthermore, libraries were spending money, perhaps needlessly, to build collections that often duplicated materials available elsewhere in the country. Congress and Secretary Henry issued Jewett's report as an appendix to the Regents' Report and distributed copies to all the libraries from which statistical information was received. Jewett proposed printing a single national catalog of all collections. The Smithsonian Institution would publish rules for the preparation of catalog entries, and libraries would submit records of their titles, ready to be duplicated. The resulting printing plates would remain at the Smithsonian for the use of any library. In Jewett's plan, the Smithsonian Institution would then publish general catalogs. Henry, seeing the direct benefit to scientists, supported Jewett in his efforts. In 1853 Jewett sought and received endorsement for the plan from the first general convention of American public librarians, assembled in New York City. Unfortunately, Jewett's plates, of Indiana clay, warped and could not be reused, and the catalog never went into production.

A complete collection of the memoirs and transactions of learned societies throughout the world and an entire series of the most important scientific and literary periodicals.
(The Act of Organization, 1846)

From the beginning, Smithsonian scientists and scholars relied heavily on books and journals to support their research. Books give scientists the substance they need for their investigations. Explorers publish their discoveries, which are verified, classified, and studied by future scholars. Library and archival collections serve to complement object collections. Artifacts gathered during the Wilkes expedition, for example, are brought into context for scholars when they are considered with secondary publications and primary resource materials, including field notes. Books in the Smithsonian Libraries offer clues to species evolution, suggest the use of machines and tools from earlier years, record the development of styles in furniture,

architecture, and other areas, and trace the beginnings of medicine, industry, and society. Books themselves may be inherently important objects, offering evidence in their content and construction of intellectual and industrial history as well as printing and design.

Throughout its history, the Smithsonian has gathered collections for its libraries, first through copyright deposit, then through international exchange, purchase, and donations. As part of the Act of Organization, Congress made the Smithsonian Institution, along with the Library of Congress, a copyright depository. Copyright law stipulated that one copy of every book produced in the United States be sent to designated institutions. Jewett used copyright deposit to build the collections, and by 1855, there were approximately 15,000 thousand volumes worth $40,000 in the library. Copyright law, however, was not truly enforceable, nor did deposit provide the type of books Henry wanted for the library. While general and popular materials added to the reading room attracted lay people, Smithsonian researchers could not rely on copyright deposit to build a good resource for scientific investigation.

Every appropriation made for publication . . . to be distributed throughout the world, is a virtual contribution to the library.
(Smithsonian Institution Annual Report, 1847)

Secretary Henry already had begun building collections through another means, one he would pursue until the Smithsonian Institution amassed a substantial scientific library. Perhaps the most important task for developing the nation's science was to acquire books and journals from more established scientific institutions in other countries, and to that end, Henry inaugurated an international exchange program for publications. It served a twofold purpose, both building the library required by legislation, but with a strong scientific focus, and presenting to the world the best work being done in the United States.

The first publication offered in exchange would be critical in legitimizing not only the new institution but also American research in the eyes of established scientific circles. Henry recognized the strong support that publication would add to the Smithsonian's pursuit of science, bringing both an international network and academic acclaim to it. The first series for distribution, the Smithsonian Contributions to Knowledge, began with *Ancient Monuments of the Mississippi Valley,* by Ephraim G. Squier and Edwin H. Davis (Washington, D.C., 1848), an early work in anthropology.

Henry sent a circular to international scientific organizations in 1847 to determine their interest in publication exchanges. In 1848 Jewett persuaded Henry to hire a London agent and compiled a list of selected publications he wanted from other societies. This can be seen as the beginning of the Smithsonian Institution exchange list, which, by 1900, was a five-hundred-page volume. In 1849 Henry and Jewett finalized the list of 173 institutions that would receive *Ancient Monuments.* Henry designed the Contributions series for scientific research and for use in exchange, and by 1852, he could declare that the value of books received from that exchange approached $5,000.

Once Henry and Jewett compiled the first lists, Jewett devoted his time to the library. Acknowledging Jewett's lack of interest, Henry placed the exchange program under his own control, essentially as an independent operation. But in 1850 Spencer Fullerton Baird, appointed as Henry's second Assistant Secretary, willingly took on management of the exchange, which he controlled throughout his tenure. Two years later, Baird informed the

Regents that the Smithsonian Institution would now distribute American scientific publications to its list of European exchange partners for any willing United States society. Within the first ten years, the Smithsonian library received four to five thousand volumes per year on exchange and within twenty years sent 383,000 pounds of exchange books abroad.

The Smithsonian's exchange network was so successful that the Librarian of Congress, Ainsworth Rand Spofford, went to Henry in 1864 with a proposal to combine the exchange efforts of the two institutions. Since his arrival as assistant librarian, three years earlier, Spofford had been working on exchange as well as cleaning up overwhelming collection backlogs at the Library of Congress. Through Spofford's efforts, the Smithsonian Institution was designated the exchange agency for all publications of the United States government, under a program called the International Exchange Service. By formalizing this official capacity, the Smithsonian strengthened its case for federal appropriations. The Brussels Convention, an international accord on publications signed in 1889, confirmed the Smithsonian Institution as America's official international exchange agent worldwide.

Exchanges primarily with scientific societies of other lands formed the nucleus of the Smithsonian Institution's research collections. Early accession books identify the breadth and scope of the scientific societies enrolled and the publications received on exchange. Periodicals and books poured in from Japan and Australia, England and Russia, and all points between. A sampling of titles includes *Proceedings of the British Association for the Advancement of Science* (Cambridge, June 1845); *The Botanical Magazine* (Botanical Society of Japan, Tokyo, 1889–1940); *A Hand-list of the*

Genera and Species of Birds (R. Bowdler Sharpe, London, 1899); *Journal of the Asiatic Society of Bengal* (Calcutta, 1850); *Essai sur la physiomonie des serpens* (H. Schlegel, Amsterdam, 1857); the Australian Museum's *History and Description of the Skeleton of a New Sperm Whale*, by William S. Wall (Sydney, 1887); and *Révision des scalidae, miocenes et pliocenes de l'Italie*, by E. de Boury (Pisa, 1890). The federal budget handsomely supported the exchange of books through the Smithsonian to the Library of Congress and to other governmental libraries, including the surgeon general's library. This support continued into the later twentieth century.

> *The Regents shall make from the interest of the fund, an appropriation not exceeding an average of $25,000 annually for the gradual formation of a library composed of valuable works pertaining to all departments of human knowledge.*
> (The Act of Organization, 1846)

Under Jewett, the Smithsonian's library expanded exponentially. While the Act of Organization called for the ongoing development of the library's collections, Secretary Henry disagreed with the spending level suggested (the entire Smithson endowment interest amounted to only $33,000 per year), which would severely curtail his plans for scientific research. While he eventually agreed to spend half the allocation, no documentary evidence shows it was ever disbursed. Secretary Henry and most of his assistants used the library as a working research collection. Jewett, however, planned on a larger scale, harking back to the congressional debate over a great national library. The library occupied an entire hall of the Smithsonian Institution Castle, and by 1850, 16,000 people visited the reading room annually. As the books and readers poured in, the library's

purpose seemed increasingly independent of Henry's goals for the Smithsonian.

Henry attempted to rein in his assistant, but by 1854 Jewett and he were at an impasse. Henry suspected Jewett's plan for a national library would consume more institutional resources, and he knew that Jewett would find support from his sponsor, Senator Choate, now a Regent, who had advocated the national library in the original congressional debate.

Jewett mounted a public campaign to force Henry to release the full amount designated for library purchases. In response, Henry fired Jewett, with the Regents' support, although the action resulted in a congressional inquiry. Choate resigned in anger from the Board of Regents. Congress again debated the Smithsonian's purpose and Henry's management, but in the end agreed that the Smithsonian would not become an independent national library.

History should forgive Jewett for his zeal in trying to build a national collection. The United States lacked a grand counterpart to the state libraries of Europe. No other library seemed eligible to be truly national in its interests. The Library of Congress had been founded to meet the needs of members, and at mid-century it was a haphazard gathering of books located in rooms in the U.S. Capitol building. Based originally on Thomas Jefferson's library, it had accumulated rapidly but randomly. No other executive branch libraries rose to prominence, leaving the United States without an official library.

William Rhees, a clerk of the Smithsonian, updated Jewett's survey of public libraries in 1859, and he reported 25,000 volumes in the Institution's library. Secretary Henry had for some time been concerned that the collections were being burdened with nonscientific material added by deposit, a concern shared, for once, by Congress, which eventually agreed to remove copyright deposit status from the Smithsonian.

> *The minerals, books, manuscripts and other property of James Smithson, which have been received by the Government of the United States, shall be preserved separate and apart from other property of the institution.*
> (The Act of Organization, 1846)

The United States government from its inception had received gifts from individuals and foreign governments and had served as the depository for collections gathered during scientific expeditions. These objects became, de facto, the national collections, and in 1858, Joseph Henry accepted responsibility for them, along with a congressional subvention of $4,000 to maintain them. The Institution's official collecting role had begun a year earlier in March 1857, as appropriately, the personal effects of James Smithson—clothing, household goods, and nearly two hundred books—were removed from the Patent Office Building and deposited in the Regents' Room at the Smithsonian Institution Building. While Smithson's personal library contained books about voyages (Weld's *Travels through the states of North America: and the provinces of Upper and Lower Canada, during the years 1795, 1796, and 1797* is one of only two titles about the Americas), his other books were those typical of a gentleman and scientist of his time. The Smithsonian Libraries still maintains the Smithson library collection today.

In 1862, when Poinsett's National Institute was dissolved, the national museum collections it had housed in the Patent Office Building were transferred to the Smithsonian Institution. Along with the specimens came Wilkes's printed reports, *Narrative of the United States Exploring Expedition . . .*

(Philadelphia: Lea and Blanchard, 1845). Henry, however, did not intend to develop a significant museum at the Smithsonian.

Wide-ranging and numerous library collections came to the Institution with scientists, curators, and explorers who did their work in its buildings or under its aegis. In 1852 J. O. Halliwell, described as a distinguished archaeologist, donated a collection of commercial, domestic, and statistical interest comprising fifty-four manuscript volumes and seven thousand separate documents dated from 1632 to 1729. The University of Jena, Germany, gave copies in 1852 of seventeenth- and eighteenth-century works by Humboldt, von Guericke, Boerhaave, and others. To celebrate Smithson's ancestry, the Duke of Northumberland, in 1859, donated works related to the history of Northumberland.

> *With reference to the collection of books . . . catalogues of all the different libraries in the United States should be procured, in order that the valuable books first purchased may be such as are not to be found in the United States.*
> (Joseph Henry, Program of Organization, 1847)

Joseph Henry's original program for the Smithsonian directed book purchases to be made for the library, specifying that "catalogues of memoirs, and of books and other materials, should be collected for rendering the Institution a center of bibliographical knowledge, whence the student may be directed to any work which he may require." Nevertheless, until modern times, book buying to build collections was less consistent and less productive than donation or exchange. The library purchased its first subject collection in 1878, when it acquired the books belonging to Professor F. B. Meek, a paleontologist and authority on fossil shells, who had lived and worked for twenty years in one room of the Castle.

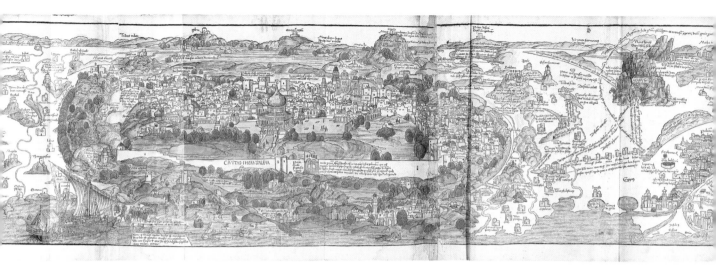

A map of Jerusalem in Bernhard von Breydenbach, *Peregrinatio in terram sanctam* (Travel to the Holy Land), 1486.

An accidental fire in the Castle in 1865 severely damaged the building, destroying the roof and consuming Smithson's personal belongings along with an important collection of paintings of Native Americans on loan to the Institution; a large library from Beaufort, South Carolina, confiscated during the Civil War; and the book collection of Bishop Johns, from Fairfax Theological Seminary, given for safekeeping by the secretary of war.

Unlike the Smithsonian, Congress had built a fireproof library stack for its collections. Secretary Henry seized the opportunity that the fire afforded to move the library out of the Castle and farther away from Smithsonian support. Working with Spofford, Henry agreed to deposit the Smithsonian collection at the Library of Congress, a plan legitimized by an act of Congress in 1866. The act authorizing the transfer contained special provisions for the Smithsonian staff to enjoy the same privileges at the Library of Congress as those accorded senators or congressmen.

Forty thousand volumes were transferred to the Library of Congress, and with them went Theodore Gill, a Smithsonian zoologist, who had been charged with care of the library among his other duties as Assistant Secretary. For many years, the Library of Congress paid part or all the salary of the Smithsonian librarian. Although most of the collection went to the Capitol, Henry retained a thousand or so books needed by Smithsonian scientists for their work. In subsequent years, the care of the remaining library collections rested with the scientific staff.

The Smithsonian Deposit, as the collection housed at the Library of Congress was named, changed the nature of the host library's collections. Spofford wrote in the 1866 annual report for the Library of Congress: "This large accession to the treasures of the library is especially valuable in the range of scientific books, comprising by far the largest collection of the journals and transactions of learned societies, foreign and domestic, which exists in America. It is also found to be an important supplement to the present library in the departments of linguistics, bibliography, statistics, voyages and travels, and works relating to the fine arts; in each of which departments it embraces works of great cost and value, while its collection of books in all branches of natural history is invaluable." The contents of the first Smithsonian Deposit are recorded in a printed list compiled by the Library of Congress at the time of the transfer. After the initial transfer, the Smithsonian continued to build its deposited collections from donations and from the International Exchange Service. In 1870 alone, more than 5,500 books were sent through the Institution to the Library of Congress. For nearly one hundred years, the Smithsonian library continued to receive serials through its exchange program and transfer them to the Library of Congress, creating long and complete sets of journals. In later years, both the Library of Congress and the Smithsonian worked to assure that at least one institution had a complete set for future researchers.

Spencer Fullerton Baird became the second Secretary in 1878, and he broadened the program of the Smithsonian to include an officially recognized national museum. Baird's childhood goal had been to assemble a major natural-history collection, and he remained an avid collector. Baird was more politically astute, perhaps, than Charles Coffin Jewett had been in pursuing a national agenda. By simultaneously gathering objects for study from numerous United States expeditions to the American West and other sources, and promoting both publications and scientific research, Baird had been expanding the range of the Institution for many years. The growth of these national collections created the need for curators. At first Baird and other Smithsonian scientists envisioned the government's collection of objects, formerly kept at the Patent Office, as specimens to be studied rather than viewed. Nevertheless, the museum's popularity with the public grew.

Henry had not succeeded in 1875 in persuading Congress to authorize construction of an addition to the nearly full Castle. The following year, as Assistant Secretary, Baird capitalized on the circumstances of the 1876 centennial exposition in Philadelphia. He secured for the Smithsonian not only displays from the United States government but also those from foreign governments and individual participants, as well as continued federal financial support for the collections. Eventually, twenty railroad cars of objects arrived on the Mall. Working with a plan presented to Congress by Gen. Montgomery C. Meigs, a civil engineer who had conducted a study of public museums in Europe, Baird, in 1877, persuaded Congress that a second building was needed to house the rapidly growing and evolving national museum. After an architectural competition, Congress authorized a building in 1879 to be known as the United States National Museum, which was completed in 1881. The Castle was renovated for multiple uses, and some of the art collections transferred at the time of the fire were returned. At the same time, according to the Smithsonian's annual report for 1880, "the corridor of the east range of the building [the Castle] has been fitted up as a reading room by the erection of reading desks on which are placed the successive numbers of certain serials as they come to hand. These, of course, comprise but a very small portion of the journals received by the Institution."

The increased activity in investigation, as well as the needs of the curators in their work of recording the history of the collections under their charge, has made it necessary to establish a working library in connection with the Museum, it being found impossible to depend upon the old method of drawing books from the Congressional Library. A small number of works

has been reclaimed from the Smithsonian Deposit in the Congressional Library, but the Museum Library is, for the most part, made up of very valuable collections of standard zoological and industrial works and bound pamphlets, composing the private library of Professor Baird, which he has given to the Museum.
(Smithsonian Institution Annual Report, 1881)

In the small library that remained after the Smithsonian Deposit was transferred, one assistant cared for the books and another prepared a catalogue of the transactions of learned societies and performed clerical duties connected with the foreign exchange system. The absence of an organized library, however, was proving detrimental to the effective study and use of specimens. At the Library of Congress, the Smithsonian Deposit grew steadily and continued to serve as the Smithsonian's primary collection; it was counted in all volume tallies into the twentieth century. The Library of Congress, though, had run out of space, and items in the deposit collections could not be easily located or retrieved. If researchers had been able to find what they needed quickly, the evolution of the Smithsonian Libraries might have followed a very different course.

Baird, in 1880, made clear his own need for an internal library along with sectional libraries, which were essentially the curators' book collections. He reported in the Smithsonian's annual report for 1880, "In view of the increasing number of employees connected with either the Smithsonian Institution, the National Museum, or the United States Fish Commission and Fishery Census Division, it was thought proper to make some provision by which some of the more interesting domestic and foreign periodicals received might be rendered easily accessible to them."

Beginning in 1880, Spencer Baird donated his own library containing works in natural history, biology, and industry; sought other collections and donations from his scientists; and renewed purchases to supplement what became the National Museum library. The librarian stationed with the Smithsonian Deposit at the Library of Congress often received a stipend from the Smithsonian Institution for care of the internal Smithsonian collection as well. Baird placed zoologist Frederick W. True in charge of the collection, and asked exchange staff to find two copies of scientific society publications, one for the deposit and one for the museum, and to obtain back issues of important periodicals. As always, the prime consideration for building collections was usefulness to the staff. During Baird's tenure, seventeen sectional libraries were developed to assist scientists in identifying objects coming into the national collections.

The Bureau of American Ethnology amassed the first sizable book collection. Congress had authorized the Smithsonian in 1879 to direct a survey of the Rocky Mountain region, and the objects brought back by the surveyors were organized into a discrete collection. The bureau was to continue the anthropological researches among North American Indians that previously had been conducted by the surveys. John Wesley Powell, whose 1869 expedition to the American Southwest was sponsored by the Smithsonian, became the director of ethnographic efforts. The library of the bureau developed quickly to support the growing science of anthropology. When, in 1909, the collections were moved into the Smithsonian Institution Building, they numbered thousands of volumes. In addition, many of the notable scientists who worked in the anthropology office gathered collections to support their work in Asia, Africa, the

Middle East, and the Pacific. These became part of the sectional library eventually known as the Smithsonian Office of Anthropology Library. The Bureau of American Ethnology remained in the Castle until 1965, when it and the Smithsonian Office of Anthropology Library moved to the National Museum of Natural History.

Not a lot is known about the early Smithsonian librarians, and the annual reports and congressional hearings offer only brief glimpses. Jane Turner, in the annual report for 1868, was said to "vindicate by her accuracy and efficiency the propriety of employing her sex in some departments of government [as she] continues to register the books as they are received through the extended system of international exchange." Twenty-two years later, the 1888 annual report noted "the resignation of Miss J. A. Turner who had for many years performed the duties of librarian with the greatest diligence and faithfulness."

Baird pursued many different scientific interests, ever widening the Smithsonian's scope of study. In 1887 he hired Samuel Pierpont Langley to build an astrophysical observatory and develop a scientific program. When Baird died that same year, Langley became the Institution's third Secretary. Langley, as early as 1896, built a steam-driven aircraft that flew unmanned, an appropriate accomplishment for the person who would see the Institution and its library into the new century.

Cyrus Adler, appointed librarian in 1892, superbly aided Langley in developing research support at the Smithsonian. Serving until 1908, Adler was almost exactly Langley's contemporary at the Institution. A professor at Johns Hopkins University, he became an honorary curator called on for occasional Smithsonian projects until 1892, when he was officially employed by the Institution as librarian. Under the direction of the two men,

the Institution and its libraries became better organized and more supportive of research. Secretary Langley drew up regulations for the conduct of the library which covered the marking of books, contents of the general collection, administration, lending, and use of library materials. According to Langley's annual report for 1880, "These books are mostly, but not exclusively, books of scientific reference, certain art serials being included among them, and though all are kept in the Secretary's office they are at the service, under certain necessary restrictions, of all connected with the Institution." To allow for easy access to collections, staff formed sectional libraries: "Sectional libraries may be formed by the Assistant Secretary, the chief Clerk, or assistant in charge, and by the curators and acting curators, and the editor. Curators and acting curators are permitted, subject to the approval of the Assistant Secretary in charge of the Museum, to form sectional libraries to be kept in their respective offices; but this shall only be done by withdrawing from the general collection such books as relate exclusively to the objects under their care." The number of sectional libraries quickly grew to thirty-five.

In testimony to Congress in 1895, the Secretary had to justify paying the salary of the librarian from Smithsonian and Library of Congress funds. Adler ably enumerated his tasks as Smithsonian librarian to the appropriations committee. By then the library (most likely including the Smithsonian Deposit) employed eight assistants.

In 1898 Adler and Langley established an employee library, although Adler worried about finding enough good books in Washington to stock it. Spencer Baird's daughter Lucy contributed general literature and periodicals to help start the new program. At the time, library staff bought books from Brentano's and other local bookstores and carefully noted their expenditures. Smithsonian internal funding and congressional appropriations for books were comparatively small but routine. Institutional accounts show that in 1886 only $1,174 of private money was spent on books.

Government regulations prohibited the purchase of manuals, newspapers, and reference books with federal appropriations unless the act for an organization specifically called for such purchases. The Smithsonian depended on annual congressional appropriations to fund book buying, which could occur only when the congressional committee inserted language in the bills to allow for it. Exceptions were allowed, but rarely. In 1898, for example, the Institution purchased former Assistant Secretary George Brown Goode's collection of scientific articles on fish to support the work of the natural history section, and later, the anthropology department bought early manuscripts for their research value.

By 1900 the National Museum received $2,000 annually from federal funds for books. That appropriation remained constant for many years. The International Exchange Service received much better funding. In 1886 the Smithsonian received $17,000 for staff to mail exchange publications; this grew to more than $25,000 by 1900. The library at the Smithsonian, called the Secretary's library or the Office library, and the library of the National Museum expanded through receipt of duplicate exchanges while still forwarding periodicals and books to the Library of Congress Smithsonian Deposit. Overcrowding at the Library of Congress generally made the deposit collections unmanageable and inaccessible for research, until the Library of Congress moved into its new building in 1897.

The astrophysical observatory organized its own library with staff that included a cataloger,

handsomely paid $900 by 1910. Its book expenditures were listed in the federal budget, and by 1890, the astrophysical library contained 12,000 volumes, enhanced by Langley's personal library on aeronautics, given after his death in 1906. In 1930 employees transferred Langley's aeronautics collection to the Smithsonian Deposit. In 1955 the observatory moved to Harvard University in a joint effort with the university's astronomy department. A large library created between the Smithsonian and Harvard continues to aid scholars.

Langley attempted to support research on many fronts. Perhaps the most curious and endearing of these was the National Zoological Park. Developed partly from the work of the zoologist William Hornaday, who gathered buffalo on the Mall in pens near the Castle, the department of living mammals grew to more than two hundred creatures and drew hundreds of visitors annually. In the Washington heat, however, the smell of live animals grew intolerable for those who worked and lived nearby. In 1889, at Langley's urging, Congress established the National Zoo. When land became available in Rock Creek Park, Langley took the opportunity to establish a more permanent home for the menagerie. The zoo developed its own library in 1898, with a separate budget for materials, a librarian, and eventually a collection of about four thousand volumes.

The National Museum named J. Elfreth Watkins as the first curator responsible for technology in 1892. Watkins, who also served briefly that year as Smithsonian librarian, donated texts on engineering and transportation to his new section. Engineering and historical collections continued to grow and coexisted with natural history specimens in the old National Museum building. From Samuel Brown's donation of alchemy books to Gen. Watts DePeyster's rare and valuable books about Napoleon, the libraries' collections were richly expanded through the generosity of donors. The DePeyster collection, which was noted for being useful in the Second World War, was transferred later to a more appropriate home at Franklin and Marshall College, in Lancaster, Pennsylvania.

The Botany Division and the U.S. National Herbarium came to the Smithsonian between 1894 and 1896. In 1905 a collection of rare botany books was added by the bequest of John Donnel Smith. Captain Smith collected rare books in beautiful bindings to complement his specimen collection from tropical America. The botany collections grew with the bequest of the library of Drs. Albert Spears Hitchcock and Agnes Chase, two curators from the department, bringing in rare books by Linnaeus and a significant collection on grasses. Curator William Dall began giving books to the mollusks sectional library in 1892. Through continued giving, until 1926, he created one of the most significant collections on the topic in the nation. Charles W. Richmond, assistant curator of birds, donated his library in 1906, a gathering rich in travel and natural history. The Lighthouse Board, which would administer the lighthouse system until July 1, 1910, and on which Joseph Henry had served, transferred the *Annales de chemie* and other titles in chemistry and physics that still remain in the National Museum of American History Library.

At the beginning of the twentieth century, the Smithsonian Institution included the zoo, the astrophysical observatory, the United States National Museum, the International Exchange Service, the Bureau of American Ethnology, and the Weather and Coastal Surveys. In addition, the Institution supported research expeditions across the globe. Objects and books were sent

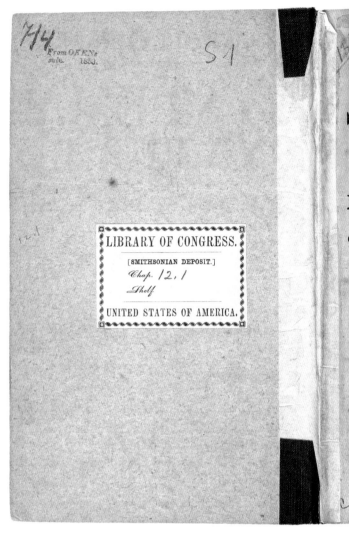

Library of Congress Smithsonian Deposit bookplate in Carolus Linnaeus, *Systema naturae* (System of nature), 1740.

to Washington in huge numbers, and the spaces allotted to the National Museum were filled to overflowing. The museum was spending about $5,000 a year on exhibits for the public and far more on building cases and cabinets for the preservation of collections.

Just so you get the books; is that it?
(William R. Wood, Chairman, Subcommittee,
House Committee on Appropriations, Hearing, 1924)

Charles Doolittle Walcott, as Secretary from 1908 to 1927, developed what is recognized as the twentieth-century Smithsonian. As a scientist, Walcott could speak to the practical aspects of research and push for academic standards that would enhance the standing of the scientific profession nationwide. Walcott developed the National Advisory Committee on Aeronautics, the forerunner of the National Aeronautics and Space Administration (NASA). He sponsored rocket scientist Robert Goddard, who received grants from the Smithsonian Institution for his early work, which was published in *The Smithsonian Institution Miscellaneous Reports,* in 1919 and 1936. Walcott oversaw the completion of the second national museum building. Although this structure houses only the National Museum of Natural History today, when it opened, in 1911, the First Ladies' gowns, the National Collection of Fine Arts, and other man-made objects were displayed in its prominent halls along with natural history specimens. The library collections supporting natural history research were moved into the new building, but a sizable collection remained in the old national museum building. By 1913 scientists like Mary Jane Rathbun, who specialized in Crustacea, were using library collections at their laboratories in Natural History to identify specimens.

The Smithsonian's involvement in the country's efforts to win the First World War took many forms. Smithsonian staff served in the war and shared their knowledge of remote locations and cultures. During the war, the U.S. Navy built a hangar behind the Castle for testing engines, and at the end of the war, when Walcott sought housing for materials collected and donated by the armed forces, Congress allowed the Smithsonian to renovate the hangar. It became a popular attraction for visitors, closing only with the development of the National Air and Space Museum in the 1970s. In 1923 Walcott opened the Freer Gallery, the gift of Detroit industrialist Charles Lang Freer, who donated his Asian and Near Eastern art collection, including a library, and the funds to construct a suitable building for it adjacent to the Castle.

Walcott lacked a librarian on a par with Adler as a champion of library service, but he himself was often an eloquent representative. Walcott's testimony to the House committees gives some sense of the state of the library and its continuing importance. In a request for two junior typists at annual salaries of $1,140 each, Walcott told the chairman: "Our situation in the library is this: For a number of years, we have been getting behind. We have a great many books given to us. We have had bequests of valuable scientific books. We have been able to incorporate part of them in the regular library and part of them have simply been stored." The library had grown through significant donations. For example, ichthyology expert Theodore Gill gave his collection on fish in 1915. Mrs. Walcott contributed books on art and architecture to the art room and the employees' library. In 1915–16 Alexander Graham Bell, the Smithsonian Regent who had accompanied Smithson's remains to the United States, donated books from his working library and 153 volumes of newspaper clippings about the Wright brothers.

When William L. Corbin became librarian in 1924, he actively sought collections that would strengthen the National Museum library. In a campaign for private funding to increase the endowments, Walcott arranged a conference on the future of the Smithsonian to coincide with the Institution's eightieth anniversary in 1927. Sadly, Walcott died before the event occurred. It went forward under Charles Abbot, the Acting Secretary. The conference highlighted Smithsonian achievements including a library display of rare and valuable scientific books. The conference proceedings called the Smithsonian library a "mine of scientific wealth" but lamented that the staff could not make full use of its resources because of lack of funding. Overall, the Regents and even the president of the United States, Calvin Coolidge, could not agree on a fundraising effort that would significantly swell the library's coffers.

In our staff we have men who are accustomed to traveling on expeditions in remote places.
(Alexander Wetmore, Subcommittee, House Committee on Appropriations, Hearing, 1945)

Charles Greeley Abbot, formerly an Assistant Secretary and the director of the astrophysical observatory, became the Smithsonian's fifth Secretary in 1928. Abbot, whose own area of research was solar radiation, supported the work of Robert Goddard, established the Division of Radiation and Organisms, now the Smithsonian Environmental

MARCUS ELIESER BLOCH, *Allgemeine Naturgeschichte der Fische* (General natural history of fishes), 1782–95.

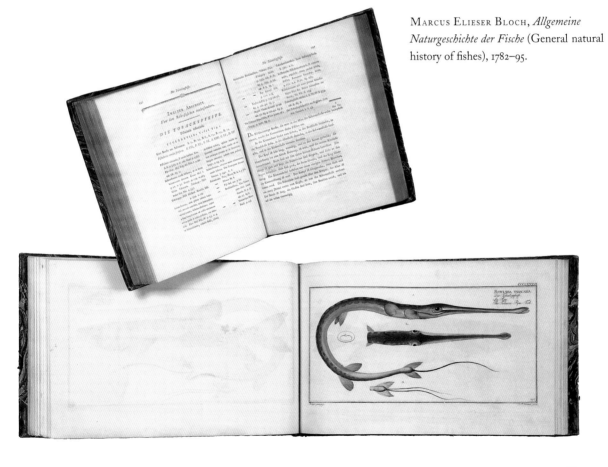

Research Center, and accepted the separately founded National Gallery of Art, then under Smithsonian oversight. In the report of the Conference on the Future of the Smithsonian Institution (February 11, 1927), the Smithsonian library was described as one of the greatest scientific libraries in the country. The Smithsonian traditionally had made research materials available to scholars, and small though the staff of the library was, it continued in this role, lending books to researchers and to other Washington laboratories. Between 1925 and 1935, the Library of Congress transferred back hundreds of volumes of natural history periodicals from the Smithsonian Deposit to complete sets in the National Museum library.

Abbot and his Assistant Secretary in charge of the United States National Museum, Alexander Wetmore, repeatedly decried the lack of funding for library operations in the 1920s. Almost yearly, Abbot and Wetmore sought funds for the library. The collections were growing through donations, but staffing did not keep pace. In 1928 Mrs. Edward H. Harriman gave a large collection on Alaska and in 1931 presented a complete set of Edward S. Curtis's *The North American Indian.* Curtis had been a member of her husband's 1899 Alaskan expedition, and Harriman became his sponsor, along with J. P. Morgan. Jesse Walter Fewkes, as chief of the Bureau of American Ethnology from 1918 to 1928, had argued years earlier for congressional support for manuscript purchases to enhance research. Anthropology expanded further with the 1932 donation of Fewkes's book collection.

In 1931 the Smithsonian requested a clerk to handle international exchanges, which were still sent to the Smithsonian Deposit at the Library of Congress. A plea for increased book funds in 1932 was repeated in 1936 and 1937. Wetmore, when questioned about a line item for publications and

binding in the 1938 budget request to Congress, made one of the earliest and clearest statements for book preservation at the Smithsonian while offering an intriguing hint at the richness of the collections: "Many of the publications that we receive for our libraries come in leaflet form. Such forms are available only for limited use. There is always danger of parts being lost unless the finished volume is bound. Once lost, the volume may be completed only at considerable expense if at all. To illustrate my meaning, here is a volume that was published in 1839, a very valuable book, the first edition of Darwin's *Journal.* It is still in the original binding and is now very much in need of repair. Something should be done with the volume before it is too late or it will be completely destroyed." In 1942 Wetmore described the museum's library as "one of the most important scientific libraries to be found in the nation. It covers the broad fields of natural science and engineering and to a lesser extent, history and art." Employees maintained the libraries with only the sketchiest of staff in the most crowded conditions. Considerations of developing collections were put aside with the beginning of the Second World War.

As had happened under Walcott, war challenged Secretary Abbot on many fronts. The military occupied the buildings on the Mall for wartime government, which forced the closing of most exhibition halls. Abbot kept the museums open on a reduced scale throughout the war, feeling that people needed to relax and continue to learn about Smithsonian subjects. He even added Sunday morning hours to allow troops passing through town to visit before shipping out.

Many valuable icons of the collections, including rare books, were moved for safety's sake outside Washington. The wartime library was under the direction of Leila Forbes Clarke, the Smithsonian's first head librarian with a degree in library science and with professional scientific expertise. Clarke, assessing relative risks, directed that the army should not evacuate the library unless the collections could be placed somewhere free of insects and mildew. Through her efforts, the collections were protected from loss and damage during their move and eventual return to the museums. Although shipments of exchange materials slowed or stopped during the war, the Smithsonian could report that by 1944 the deposit contained about 600,000 volumes and the library collections included 200,000 volumes. The libraries continued to receive significant donations such as that of automaker Ralph G. Packard, who donated his collection of books on arms and armor in 1942.

When, near the end of the war, Abbot resigned to return to his own research, Wetmore was chosen to succeed him. While he continued to advocate library support and the addition of staff positions for the library, Wetmore turned his attention to the creation of a new museum celebrating achievements in air flight, which had been mandated by Congress at the end of the war. As had happened after the First World War, there was no place to hold all the wartime memorabilia donated to the Institution. The hangar on the grounds of the Castle still served as the flight museum, but it quickly became too popular to sustain the crowds that visited it.

Congress in 1946 transferred to the Smithsonian and Wetmore, an ornithologist, the Canal Zone Biological Area in Panama. Smithsonian researchers began studying the Panamanian environment during canal construction, establishing a small station in 1923 that expanded to cover all aspects of tropical biology. Now, as the Smithsonian Tropical Research Institute (STRI), its work includes the environmental sciences. The Canal Zone library developed into the STRI library, a large, modern research facility in Panama City used by students of the University of Panama and researchers throughout Central America.

The hundredth anniversary of the founding of the Institution was commemorated and celebrated in 1946 with participation from all Smithsonian museums and the library. Leila Clarke contributed a history of the library to a commemorative issue of *Science Magazine*. By this time, library collections were found throughout the Institution, in organized branch collections and in offices in all buildings of the Smithsonian. Books continued to go to the Library of Congress for the deposit; occasionally books returned from the Library of Congress to the museums. Library staff and collections supported all the subjects of the National Museum, which comprised the divisions of anthropology, geology, biology, engineering and industry, and American history.

I am convinced that the Library's passive acceptance of a long-continuing policy of "make it do, do without" is a bad thing because of its serious effect on the scientific work of the Institution.
(Leila Clarke to Alexander Wetmore, 1951)

In continued pleas for congressional funding, Secretary Wetmore cited dust and dirt and backlogs in the library, and sought every kind of assistance by asking for librarians and catalogers, cleaners and messengers.

The Smithsonian's academic status prompted congressional scrutiny during the beginning of the Cold War, and the library was not exempt from suspicion. Despite a shutdown of most communication between the United States and the Soviet Union, library-to-library exchanges continued even when official cooperative programs failed. During the 1950 congressional hearings, the chair of the subcommittee on appropriations asked Wetmore if the Russians still participated in the International Exchange Service. Wetmore, who both urged and supported continuing study of Russian science, admitted that the Soviets did not take part in the official exchange but "the library does receive publications direct from [the Soviet Union] and we know from inquiry that various institutions do the same."

In 1951 Secretary Wetmore reorganized and centralized the Smithsonian libraries. The offices of the Secretary's library and the National Museum library were combined into the Office of the Librarian and moved to the Smithsonian Castle. By 1952 the staffing situation grew desperate. The government severely cut the number of federal employees across the board, and accordingly the libraries were forced to reduce service to many areas, including withdrawing the entire staff from the fine arts sectional library.

> *Carmichael was never particularly sympathetic to . . . the plight of the Smithsonian libraries: He had to be convinced that the Library of Congress was not the best place for housing early scientific descriptions and reports that were needed in ongoing research.*
> (James Conaway, *The Smithsonian: 150 Years of Adventure, Discovery, and Wonder,* 1995)

Wetmore retired at the end of 1952, and the new Secretary, Leonard Carmichael, formerly the president of Tufts University and a psychologist, at first may have shown a managerial conservatism in response to governmental austerity. Nevertheless, Carmichael eventually oversaw a major expansion of buildings and programs. Secretary Carmichael planned and successfully persuaded Congress to establish the Museum of History and Technology and the National Collection of Fine Arts/National Portrait Gallery, as well as long-awaited wings for

the Natural History building to meet the need for collections and research space. The libraries, under the direction of a series of professionally trained librarians, began sorting their collections in the early 1950s in preparation for stocking the library to be established at the Museum of History and Technology under the direct supervision of the Office of the Librarian. In 1953 the Library of Congress and the Smithsonian negotiated a permanent transfer to the Library of Congress of the Smithsonian Deposit, which was now too large to keep efficiently and effectively as an entity separate from the rest of the library's collections. Smithsonian staff retained certain rights to borrow materials and had access to the library stacks until, almost forty years later, security concerns led to restrictions on access even for Library of Congress staff.

Secretary Carmichael's controversial decision to transfer the deposit to the Library of Congress was forced by inescapable administrative issues. The Smithsonian could not continue dual collections indefinitely, particularly in a period of strained resources. Carmichael's entreaties to Congress in 1964 echo those of earlier secretaries and highlight the library's contributions: "I always hate to ask for any addition in administrative services and yet it is necessary, with our accelerated programs, with this new building, with the work in art, these scientific programs that I have spoken to you about, with our need for an increase in the library, which is a working library—we let the public in, but our library is primarily to make it possible for our own staff to do its job. I said we had answered 400,000 queries. The library was important in helping with this work." Carmichael appreciated the library's potential in building resources through donations. In the 1950s the library added five gift collections of research materials, leading the Secretary to

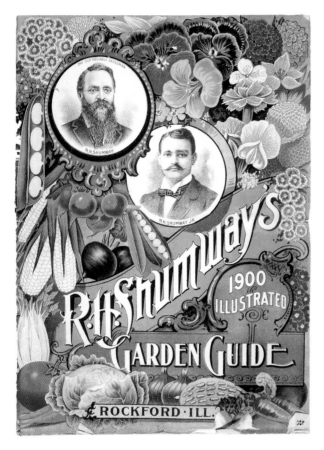

R.H. Shumway's 1900 Illustrated Garden Guide, 1900.

conclude, "the ability to attract donors remains an essential characteristic of the libraries."

The American History library received two notable collections in 1952, those of philatelist Franklin B. Bruns and army commander John J. Pershing. In 1959 Columbia University and Harvard University gave the Smithsonian large trade-literature collections. Trade catalogs, important for the study of commercial America, identify objects and their use, document the development of American manufacturing and marketing, and provide visual evidence of the tastes and practices of earlier times. The Smithsonian Institution Libraries now maintains the largest such collection in the country, with 285,000 items representing more than 30,000 companies. The Libraries has

built on this strength by accepting, in 1988, the Heinz trade-catalog collection, which features machine-tool catalogs, and by purchasing, in 1989, a large portion of the trade-catalog collection of the Franklin Institute of Philadelphia.

> *Still ahead, but very much in the libraries' future, is work on a system for the integration of files of information in the literature with those pertaining to specimens and artifacts in the museums to create a totally responsive and integrated information storage and retrieval system.*
>
> (S. Dillon Ripley, Annual Report to the Regents, 1969)

S. Dillon Ripley, Secretary of the Smithsonian from 1964 to 1984, greatly enhanced the public image of the Institution and its libraries during his tenure. The first evidence of his imaginative style came with the opening of the Museum of History and Technology (now the National Museum of American History, Behring Center). Although the museum was built under his predecessors, Ripley planned a showcase of public events of the sort that would define the Smithsonian for the next two decades. Ripley's energy and enthusiasm, combined with his ability to capitalize on public relations opportunities, broadened the Institution's appeal to an appreciative public. He presided over the construction of the Hirshhorn Museum and Sculpture Garden; the opening of the National Air and Space Museum; the creation of The Smithsonian Associates, the Smithsonian Environmental Research Center on the Chesapeake Bay, and the Cooper-Hewitt National Design Museum in New York City; the transfer of the African Art Museum to Smithsonian stewardship; and the planning for a new Asian art museum to house the Arthur M. Sackler collection. The African art library immediately became a major resource for institutions and individuals worldwide. In addition, Secretary Ripley promoted the beginning of the American Folklife Festival (1967) and many grant-making programs engendered by the National Museum Act (first funded in 1972, to enable museums to serve the public and to protect national treasures).

For all his public showmanship, Ripley was a great advocate and supporter of a strong research library. With the expansion in the number of museums and research institutes, each new facility planned space for its library, allowing Smithsonian researchers to benefit from the proximity of books to objects. In 1967 the Smithsonian established a strong presence in New York City by accepting the Cooper-Hewitt Museum, formerly part of the Cooper Union, and along with its decorative arts and design collections, its noteworthy library. The Hewitt sisters had supervised the library for almost thirty years, and when it moved to the Andrew Carnegie mansion on East 91st Street, the Smithsonian's new venue for the collections, many older catalog cards bore the note "shelved in Miss Hewitt's office." Today, as the library for the National Design Museum, the Cooper-Hewitt library is home to a graduate program and the chief resource for a burgeoning number of New York designers.

By the late 1960s the Smithsonian had become a multifaceted, diverse organization. Its fragmented library system, however, could not provide the service required in support of new programs. In 1968 the Secretary created a new structure, formally known as the Smithsonian Institution Libraries, that could more easily respond to changes. Ripley hired Russell Shank, an eminent librarian from Columbia University, as its first director. Ripley described the inadequacies of the Institution's library services during House appropriations hearings: "The Smithsonian Institution is ranked

Illustration from a catalog of the Boston Rubber Shoe Company [1895?].

rather highly among major libraries in the Washington area with total of 750,000 volumes and an enormously poor ratio of staff to volumes. . . . Library funding and staffing are subminimal. There is of course a long record of woe and distress regarding the Smithsonian Libraries and I am not revealing anything new. . . . Over a series of years the library must be kept at a sort of steady state if not improved, and we have not been able to do that at the Smithsonian Institution."

When previous secretaries assured Congress that the Smithsonian Institution was the best scientific library in Washington, the country, and maybe the world, they were referring to the Smithsonian Deposit collection as well as the Smithsonian Institution library. Now, with the establishment of a centrally administered but decentralized system, the Smithsonian Institution Libraries could provide highly sophisticated services to the curatorial staff. At the beginning of the Ripley/Shank years, there were fewer than 600,000 volumes in the collections of the Smithsonian Libraries. To support the rapidly evolving programs of the Institution, in the next four years, librarians added more than 60,000 volumes to the collections. But the staff needed to organize the collections, particularly in the centralized functions of acquisitions, cataloging, and binding, did not accompany that growth. Future secretaries and directors would have to address modernizing, cataloging, rehousing and cleaning, and preserving the collections.

Secretary Ripley's vision for the Libraries included automation, which had been only barely introduced into the Smithsonian and then mostly in scientific fields. Under Shank's direction, library staff showed that they could adapt to and use automation by designing an automated serials purchase system and beginning data input for machine-readable records. They turned that ability to cataloging and controlling the widely dispersed collections. For many years, Smithsonian librarians used the Dewey decimal system to organize books. In order to cope with the increased size of the collections, in the 1950s Smithsonian catalogers adopted the Library of Congress classification scheme, which allowed for more rapid cataloging. Recognizing the potential in automated library systems, the Smithsonian Institution Libraries became the first federal library to participate in shared automated cataloging through the Online Computer Library Center (OCLC) network. The branches of the Libraries finally achieved unity across the Institution with their first fully automated integrated system in 1983. With automation, the Libraries' catalog was available to researchers from any branch and, eventually, from their desks.

While the Institution's collections and programs grew, the work of caring for collections did not

keep pace, and accounts of trying to dust and shift books during many moves fill both annual reports and congressional hearings. The museum buildings remained without air-conditioning until the 1950s, and objects and employees alike battled dust, heat, and humidity in summer. Winter conditions were no better, as dry winter air and drafts also wreaked havoc. Over time the director of the Libraries took many steps to improve the physical condition of the collections. Existing libraries were renovated as funding permitted. The Museum of History and Technology library established the pattern for the future by providing a full service library within the museum. As the museums and research institutes acquired greater complexity, the Libraries adopted an increasing sophistication in its range of services.

While many noteworthy donations that formed subject libraries came from Smithsonian employees, some of the greatest contributions came from private individuals who wished to enrich the nation and its cultural holdings. In 1974 the Dibner Library of the History of Science and Technology, the largest special collection within the Smithsonian Libraries, was established with a gift to the nation of more than ten thousand books, manuscripts, and objects from the Burndy Library. Established in 1936 in Norwalk, Connecticut, the Burndy Library was the achievement of Bern Dibner, an electrical engineer and collector of books on the history of science, particularly electricity. Dibner envisioned the collection as the heart of a center for the study and presentation of the history of science and technology located in the National Museum of History and Technology. After twenty-five years, the number of scholars, exhibitions, symposia, and books gathered under or served by the Dibner Library of the History of Science and Technology testifies to both keen foresight and dedication in realizing his vision. The collection is particularly strong in the theoretical journeys of mathematics, physics, chemistry, and astronomy and includes the work of major figures such as Isaac Newton, Galileo, Copernicus, Euclid, Albert Einstein, and Marie Curie.

The Burndy Library gift helped to focus attention on the Smithsonian's rare books collections, which are now organized into discrete locations in the National Air and Space Museum, the Cooper-Hewitt National Design Museum in New York City, the National Museum of American History, and the National Museum of Natural History. These collections have been enhanced by many major gifts. The family of John Phipps, investor and amateur naturalist, donated rare illustrated books on birds, especially by Gould and Elliot, in 1980 to honor Secretary Ripley. The Bella Landauer sheet music collection, focused on aeronautical themes, brought a specialized dimension to the Libraries' collections. The Marcia Brady Tucker donation of ornithology books, with support from the next generation of the family, is being digitized and shared with the public on the Internet. Claire Marton and her husband, colleagues of the Curies, spent their retirement years as volunteers at the Smithsonian and left their considerable collection of books in the history of physics to the Libraries.

While the unprecedented expansion of the Smithsonian stopped after Secretary Ripley's retirement, subsequent years have been exciting for the Institution and the Libraries. Robert McCormick Adams, a scholar and anthropologist-educator, embraced the public education mission of the Smithsonian as its ninth Secretary. Under his direction, scientific research and publication also expanded, as did the scholars' program of the Institution. The Smithsonian Libraries developed

policies to govern the continuity and consistency of service, which, along with commensurate advances in the professionalism of its librarians, raised its visibility within the Institution and nationally. The International Exchange Service, which had continued to operate its own administrative office well into the 1980s, was transferred to the Smithsonian Libraries and finally disbanded in the early 1990s, when it had clearly outlived its purpose.

When the Institution concluded negotiations in 1989 with the George Gustav Heye Foundation to accession its premier collection of Native American holdings, planning began for the National Museum of the American Indian library and for greater subject strength in Native American materials. Since then, superb collections, such as the Lloyd and Charlotte Wineland collection of Native American and Western Exploration, a major resource for the study of Native American culture, have been added.

One permanent legacy of Smithsonian participation in many world's fairs and international expositions between 1876 and 1914 is a substantial collection of publications and memorabilia. World's fairs serve historians as snapshots of Western culture at a given point in time. Publications deriving from them record technological advances, industrial achievements, and popular entertainment. The world's fair holdings were enhanced by the addition of the collection of Edward J. Orth, who gathered materials for fifty years, beginning with the 1939 New York fair. In 1989 the Smithsonian Libraries received printed materials from the Larry Zim World's Fair collection, which brought significant publications dating from the 1851 Great Exhibition to the 1986 Vancouver World Exposition.

The Smithsonian Libraries, during the Adams years, developed a preservation services unit,

"Noápeh. An Assiniboin Indian. Psíhdja-Sáhpa. A Yanktonan Indian," plate 12 from MAXIMILIAN PRINZ VON WIED, *Reise in das innere Nord-America in den Jahren 1832 bis 1834* (Trip to North America between the years 1832 and 1834), 1839–41.

primarily to deal with hundreds of thousands of nineteenth-century books printed on brittle paper. Previously, library conservators repaired rare and valuable books, rebinding them and preparing items for exhibition. Through reformatting, micro-filming, and preservation treatments such as de-acidifying and enhanced environmental controls, the Libraries staff works to save all the Smith-sonian's printed books and manuscripts for future generations.

When Adams returned to teaching in 1994, he left the task of opening the National Museum of the American Indian to his successor, I. Michael Heyman, formerly of the University of California at Berkeley. With Heyman's support, the Smith-sonian Libraries began a strong fund-raising program and increased the use of automation. Barbara J. Smith, Libraries director from 1989 to 1994, led efforts to bring the Internet and online services to the Institution and launched fund-raising efforts for the Libraries.

When the Smithsonian celebrated its 150th birthday on August 10, 1996, the Libraries played a major role both through the participation efforts of the staff in celebratory events and by developing the exhibition "From Smithson to Smithsonian: The Birth of an Institution" (online version at www.sil.si.edu). Today the Smithsonian Institution Libraries comprises twenty-two libraries in a unified system offering service to Smithsonian staff, researchers, and the public. Efforts to reach the public and share national treasures include book exhibitions, lectures, special events, and digi-tal publications and scholarly editions. With grants from internal funds, the Smithsonian Libraries in 1999 established its Imaging Center under present director Nancy E. Gwinn. The center makes elec-tronic versions of rare and significant books, and as a result, the content of the book itself is available on the Internet to researchers and public alike.

The Libraries maintains exchanges with more than four thousand institutions worldwide, which continue to supply Smithsonian scientists with important scientific periodicals. In the twenty-first century, Smithsonian catalogers work with meta-data to make websites as accessible as books on the shelf. Preservation programs help to ensure the continued use of materials in the collections, and library staff make the collections accessible to each visitor in the best and most responsible way possible.

The Smithsonian Libraries participates today in the advancement of science and the arts, just as it has done from the inception of the Institution. Sometimes a seemingly invisible entity, the Smithsonian Institution Libraries, through the exchange program, secured important scientific periodicals for the country. Librarians have sent books, in turn, to other libraries and other lands. The role of the Libraries vis-à-vis the Institution, the government, universities, and the American people has grown, changing to meet the needs of the times. Serving as both a public and an academic library, a scholarly resource and general service, the Libraries offers a galaxy of resources navigable by anyone, via the Internet or in person. The Smithsonian Libraries contains books dating from the thirteenth century to the present, books bound in vellum and encrypted on disks, books on insects, flowers, steam engines, and rockets. Exploring these treasures is well worth the journey.

Mary Augusta Thomas is Assistant Director, Management and Technical Services Division, Smithsonian Institution Libraries, and the exhibition curator for An Odyssey in Print: Adventures in the Smithsonian Libraries.

Book Conservation Laboratory, Smithsonian Institution Libraries. Photo: © 1999 Jon Goell.

On Cranium of Ratitae, See Parker, 1866, Phil. Trans. 113

Note on the method of incubation among the birds of the order Struth-
ones. Sci P.Z.S 1866, 232.

Observations sur l'Epiornis maximus, Bianconi, R.Z. 1865, 47 (near Succottanfia!
On the plumage of Dinornis Robustus ⟨D allas Ann. Mag. 1865, 66 figs. 2.3
Notice of a more complete Skeleton of ⟩ ⟨Allis, Nat. Hist Rev. 1864, 1865, 636
Dinornis Journ. Proc. Linn. Soc. VIII, 1866, 55. ⟩ Zool. Soc. p. 9195-7.

On Dinornis, pt. IX, Owen, Tr. Z.S. 1867, 337, pls. 63, 4, 5, 6.
  "   "   robustus + Owen P.Z.S. 1867, 881; Hector, P.Z.S. 1867, 991 (Egg.)
  " Cnemiornis Calcitrans Owen Tr. Z.S. 1867, 395, pls. 63-4-5-6-7.
  " Aepyornis, Joly R.Z. 1867, 337. — Comptes Rendus XXV, 1867, 476.
  "   "   Rowley, P.Z.S. 1867, 892.   ⟨On Dinornithidae, various
  "   "   Grmididaer, Ibis, 1866, 65 (egg-birds)   papers, Trans. Zool. Soc. 1869-71
  "   "   Milne E. + Grandid., Ann. Mag. IV.H. 1869
             801, from Compt. Rend. 1869, p. 801.
  "   "   Nathusius, Z. wiss. Zool. 1871, 330 Egg
  "   "   Yule "Marco Polo" egg fig.
             Bianconi C.R. 1869, 162
Dinornis, Owen, Tr. Z.S. VIII, 119, pl.19.   XIV-XVI. [see back Two flyleaves]
Aepyornis back two fly leaves

AVES.

Order VI. STRUTHIONES, *Lath.*

Fam. I. **STRUTHIONIDÆ**, *Vig.* 1825. Anatomy; Macalister, Proc. Roy. Irith Soc. IX, pp 1-24

Subfam. I. **Struthioninæ**, *G. R. Gr.* 1840 *et Bp.* 1849.

2458. STRUTHIO, *L.* 1735.
  G. of B. iii. p. 526, pl. 138. 4; *Reich. S. A.* t. 32. f.

9841. **camelus**, *L.*; *P. E.* 457; *Trans. Z. S.* iv. pl. 67, a.   Syrian & Arabian
  australis, *Gurney.*   Dsrts., N. Afr.
  ? epoasticus, *Bp.*; *Schl. De Dier.* fig. p. 236 ?   S. Africa white nile see Stugl. Russ 347
  *   N. Afr. Marno, Zool. Gart. 1865, 2

Fam. II. **RHEIDÆ**, *A. Newt.* 1868.

Subfam. I. **Rheinæ**, *Bp.* 1849.

2459. RHEA, *Moehr.* 1752. Cunningham, P.Z.S. 1871, 105, pl. 6, 6ª (Osteolog.)
  Touyou, *Cuv.* 1797-98.
  Tuyus, *Rafinq.* 1815.
  G. of B. iii. p. 527, pl. 138. 5; *Reich. S. A.* t. 32. f.

a. RHEA.

9842. **americana**, *Lath.*; *Knowsl. Menag.* pl.; *Pr. Z. S.* 1860,   N. Patagonia,
  fig. p. 208; *Trans. Z. S.* iv. pl. 68.   La Plata to S.
  rhea, *L.*   of Rio Negro.

*****2458**ª. Autruchon, *Tem.* 18 ?

9841ª. ? bidactylus, *Tem.* (L'Autruchon).   Int. of Africa,
                                                                            ? Fazogloa near
                                                                            Djebel Dul.

B

Annotated page from GEORGE ROBERT GRAY, *Hand-list of the Genera and Species of Birds . . .*
in the British Museum (Natural History), 1869–71.

The Curator and the Book / Storrs L. Olson

*W*here I work, in a natural history museum, a curator's life is tied to his or her collection of specimens. In my case, it is specimens of birds, and of fossil birds as well. For others, it might be fishes, mollusks, mosses, beetles, or shrimp. Our purpose and our inspiration come in large measure from the knowledge we can derive from these specimens. Yet all too frequently we experience days when we are kept from our specimens and collections by other duties—refereeing manuscripts of colleagues, revising our own manuscripts, writing or reviewing grant proposals, answering queries from colleagues and the public, and dealing with administrative trivia. We often lament too many days spent without handling specimens—but no day passes in the museum when we do not consult a book.

The librarians asked me to contribute my perspective—not that of a reader of books that the critic must be—nor that of the keeper and arranger of books as a librarian must be, but that of a user of books that the scientist must be. And books are absolutely necessary to everything we do as scientists.

Books and libraries are as essential to a researcher as land and a plow to a farmer, flour and an oven to a baker, or stays and quiddities to a lawyer. Libraries are the repositories of most of what has been learned before. Without research in libraries we would find ourselves repeating the work of others and rediscovering facts already long known (which happens often enough as it is). But books are not merely the tools but also the product of research scientists, just as wheat and loaves are the products of farmers and bakers. We create them and use them, and like the baker eating of his own loaf, we use what we ourselves create. After some forty years of publishing scientific papers, I cannot begin to remember everything I have written, so I consult my own papers as much as or more than anyone else. Museum research begins and ends with books.

I consider myself fortunate that my interests are diverse and my research interdisciplinary, so that I have frequent use of the specialist libraries throughout the Smithsonian Institution's Museum of Natural History in addition to the museum's general library collection and that in the Division

The Libraries' Charles Coffin Jewett Room, Arts and Industries Building, Smithsonian Institution. Office of Imaging, Printing, and Photographic Services, Smithsonian Institution.

of Birds. I regularly visit the libraries in Mollusks, Anthropology, Mammals, Botany, and Amphibians and Reptiles, and pay less frequent visits to Entomology, Fishes, and Crustacea. Each of these little chapels of knowledge has its own aura and history, although because of staffing shortages, the library administration finds it difficult to manage so many scattered collections. From time to time, the suggestion is put forth to consolidate these smaller libraries, but the curators and other users scarcely allow the subject to be entertained.

Scientists are adamant about keeping what they consider to be *their* books close to their offices and specimens. These are very much working libraries, and they just don't work as well if they are not physically close to one's specimens. Books are so indispensable to the museum scientist that each curator will necessarily have a personal research library in his or her office (and probably at home as well). Many of the curator's personal books are redundant with the Smithsonian's holdings, either

having been obtained prior to the curator's coming to the Institution or being of such importance that a personal copy is needed for annotations or to prevent repeated trips to a more distant source. A curator may possess other volumes lacking in the Smithsonian collections, and many of these are eventually given to the Smithsonian Libraries by curators with concerns for posterity.

Acquisitive curators with active bibliographical interests accumulated some of the Smithsonian's most useful and important collections. In the Division of Birds, Charles W. Richmond devoted much of his efforts in the first decades of the twentieth century to straightening out details of avian nomenclature. In the process, he sought out antiquarian book dealers throughout North America and Europe and purchased hundreds of obscure and recondite volumes critical to his inquiries. That he was able to do so on a curator's salary reflects not only that he was a bachelor but also that such desiderata were then much more readily available and relatively inexpensive. Now, much of what Richmond donated to the Smithsonian Libraries is prohibitively expensive or unobtainable. With increasing frequency, cherished tomes that were once only a few steps away are removed to the rare book facility for preservation and greater security. They remain readily available, however, and far more so than if they had been stolen or destroyed through misuse.

Division of Birds staff and visitors usually eat lunch at a big table in the divisional library, a practice not unknown elsewhere in the museum, as in the library in Amphibians and Reptiles. This is another source of mild consternation to some fastidious librarians, but it is a tradition that, at least in Birds, must go back nearly a century, if not longer.

And where better to take one's repast than surrounded by beloved books? Scarcely a lunch passes that I do not reflect on the thirty-six volumes of the *Nouveau dictionnaire d'histoire naturelle* across from me. This set once belonged to curator J. Harvey Riley and is now a little the worse for wear, with some of the spines loose or lacking. It duplicates another set held in the Smithsonian's Dibner Library. Why, one might ask, is such a general encyclopedia, published from 1816 to 1819 and now very much outdated in most respects, in the library of the Division of Birds? Because it is packed with original articles about birds by Louis Jean Pierre Vieillot which contain hundreds of then-new scientific names, a great many of which are still in use. Relatively little is known about Vieillot's life, yet his contribution to ornithology was immense. He named more new species of North American birds than either Audubon or Alexander Wilson. Looking at those tattered tomes of the *Dictionnaire* over lunch never fails to make me wish I had the time to compile a proper index to Vieillot's contributions within it.

As with the *Nouveau dictionnaire,* most books of scientific research were never meant to be read as one would read a novel. Instead they are storehouses of information. If I encounter a scientific name for a bird that has not been used for more than a century, I will open one or two or three books for a few seconds each to determine what name is used today for that same bird. The description of a new species of crayfish may detail every bristle on every segment of its many appendages and never be read by anyone save its author until a related new species is discovered that needs to be compared and documented. And then the scientist expects to have the book containing the first description readily at hand.

Just as a thousand ships were launched by Helen of Troy's face, a thousand metaphorical scientific voyages might be launched by a brief article in a scientific journal. The classic example would be Watson and Crick's single-page note titled "A structure for deoxyribose nucleic acid," which appeared in the magazine *Nature* on April 2, 1953 (vol. 171: 737–38). Renowned for its succinctness and understatement, this Nobel-winning article launched an uncountable number of studies of the DNA molecule, an enterprise that dominates the life sciences today. Museum systematists, myself included, who formerly relied almost entirely on anatomy to determine the interrelationships of animals and plants, have been dragged, often kicking and screaming, into the biochemical age and increasingly have had to admit the utility of molecular technology in their studies.

In the course of composing the preceding paragraph, I went with some trepidation to the Natural History branch library with the idea of looking at Watson and Crick's original paper, knowing what I might find. My apprehension was fully realized when I opened that volume of *Nature* and found that the desired (and desirable) page had been razored out, only to be replaced with a rather nasty old photocopy. Such vandalism is the bane of both the librarian and the book user, but it is impossible to anticipate and protect every page that might come to have commercial or historical appeal lest the entire library be locked away and made less functional. We can only wish for the inventiveness of a Dante Alighieri to conjure up a place in hell horrible enough to do justice to thieves and defacers of books.

But we must exercise caution as to who is to be condemned among the latter, for we must exclude the careful annotator of books, who may actually enhance the utility of a volume by noting errors or additions. One of the most useful publications for the museum ornithologist is the twenty-seven-volume *Catalogue of the Birds in the British Museum*, issued from 1874 to 1895. Far more than what the title suggests, these volumes contain descriptions of every species of bird then known, plus synonymies of all their scientific names and their references. Thus it is an indispensable guide to the earlier literature of ornithology—but far from perfect.

In the Division of Birds library there are at least two sets of the *"Cat. Bds.,"* and by far the most useful is the working copy that has in it the annotations of generations of curators and other users who have penciled in corrections to the errors and omissions they have come across. I well remember trying to track down a seemingly intractable detail of nomenclature and in turning to the working set of the *Catalogue* found an annotation that solved the whole issue. There is no way to estimate how long it would have taken me to find the solution otherwise. There must be hundreds of other instances in which the Smithsonian's copy of a volume has scientific or historical value beyond that of any other copy in existence.

James Smithson (1765–1829) by Henri-Joseph Johns, 1816. National Portrait Gallery, Smithsonian Institution.

It is handy to have a duplicate backup such as the British Museum *Catalogue* for photocopying or when pages or plates might be missing from the first set, although some might begrudge the shelf space it occupies. This brings up another sometimes thorny issue—that of duplicates in general throughout the library system. The librarian sees an advantage in consolidating all the smaller divisional collections in making the many duplicate volumes redundant and disposable. But, again, these are working libraries, and certain general works are so indispensable that the divisions must have their own copies close at hand.

For example, the *Proceedings of the Zoological Society of London* published in the last half of the nineteenth century are so important for descriptions of new animal species that any good systematist usually refers repeatedly to the *PZS*. Consequently there are at least four sets in the Smithsonian Libraries. We do not have one in the Division of Birds, but until recently the set in Mollusks, immediately below my office, was closer to me than the Birds library. Then the Division of Mollusks was moved to the west wing of the building, and now I bridle at having to walk all the way over to Mammals to consult their set. How spoiled we get here sometimes.

The books that curators most frequently use are prosaic scientific journals in library buckram or tattered catalogs of scientific names in moldering half-calf that leaves smudges on the hands. But we also have a very real need for the vellum-wrapped incunabula and lavish gilt-edged folios of hand-colored lithographs. Admired for their historical importance, rarity, and intrinsic aesthetic qualities, they are essential for the knowledge they contain.

My research has dealt heavily with extinct birds from islands, and I have made numerous rewarding voyages of my own to some very remote destinations. Species of birds on the islands of the world have been going extinct rapidly ever since humans began to colonize. Many early voyages to the Pacific, for example, recorded birds that have never been encountered again. Some of these might be represented in museum collections by a specimen or two; others might be known only by a drawing or a description. To determine the origins of some of these species, I have spent many hours poring over the accounts and itineraries of ancient voyages of exploration.

Naturalists on early voyages collected and described many new shells, and the Mollusk library has an especially fine collection of volumes from their explorations. Among these wonderful old books, one can fairly sense the ghost of curator William Healey Dall, one of the Smithsonian's preeminent malacologists, who was instrumental in obtaining scores of these important works.

Many of the most precious holdings in the Smithsonian Libraries are too dear for the pocketbook of any curator or even the Institution itself but have come to us through the foresight and generosity of magnanimous donors. I am privileged to consider that I have a remote but special connection to some of these works.

I grew up in Tallahassee, Florida, and Lake Jackson, north of town, was one of the prime hunting and fishing destinations for my high school associates and me. One of the choicest pieces of real estate in all of North Florida is Ayavalla Plantation, some ten square miles of field and forest around the north end of the lake, then owned by John H. Phipps. My cohorts and I assiduously stalked the peripheries of Ayavalla in search of game, perhaps envious of the landholders but always grateful that they were preserving native habitats in the face of rampant real estate development.

One April day in 1965, by chance my twenty-first birthday, I collected a duck on Lake Jackson in a plumage seldom encountered away from its Canadian breeding grounds. Just after I had waded back to dry land (not Phipps's) with my prize, a boat came roaring up and a gruff old fisherman with one eye squinted shut stalked up and demanded to see my "permissions." It was old "Ben" Phipps himself. I was more than a little relieved to be able to produce from my billfold wrinkled copies of both state and federal collecting permits. This mollified Mr. Phipps, who resumed his fishing. It was my only encounter with the seigneur of Ayavalla, but figuring that he was a witness to the circumstances of collection of the specimen, I added his name to the label and catalog as one of the collectors.

Fifteen years after the above incident took place, when I had been a curator at the Natural History Museum for about five years, John H. Phipps donated to the Smithsonian Libraries fifty-six magnificent volumes, mostly on birds and emphasizing the treasured works of John Gould. Over the years when I have consulted any of these books, I have always recalled my fortuitous link with their former owner and fond memories of my North Florida boyhood. Books are so often much more than collections of words and pictures.

Great voyages of discovery often resulted in magnificent volumes, intended to impress, that described and illustrated the scenery, peoples, and objects of natural history encountered by the explorers. But perhaps it is not as well appreciated that, in an age of great volumes, the potential of producing a sumptuous book at times provided the impetus for voyages and collecting expeditions. One of the most remarkable instances of this is the Australian sojourn of John Gould. Gould, with much assistance from his wife and other illustrators and colorists, made his living by producing and selling through subscription magnificent folio volumes mainly about birds. In May 1838 he packed himself and his family off to Australia, where they lived (and multiplied) for nearly two years. During this time Gould himself collected specimens widely while also relying on his own collectors, such as the industrious but ill-fated John Gilbert, and a network of government officials and other residents who obtained specimens for him.

This resulted in the discovery of dozens of new species of birds and mammals that Gould himself described in short articles in scientific journals. The subscribed works that came out of Gould's Australian venture include his monograph on kangaroos, the seven-volume *Birds of Australia,*

Thomas Gilbert Pearson, *The Bird Study Book,* 1917.

which, with its supplement, contain some six hundred hand-colored plates, and the three-volume *Mammals of Australia.* It was the prospect of creating these books that sent Gould and his family off on their voyage of exploration and poor Gilbert to his death at the hands of aborigines in the Australian desert in June 1845.

I cannot close and leave the impression, as I may have done, that there is any lasting tension between curators and librarians. Nothing could be further from the truth. Given that members of the two groups usually have very different training, backgrounds, and perspectives, our interrelationships are actually remarkably harmonious. The foibles of librarians are very scarce and tame by comparison with the copious and egregious foibles of an entire natural history museum's assortment of curators. And our librarians must deal with them all.

Our librarians are among the most patient and helpful people on the planet. There is no topic, from sedimentology to sea urchins, for which they are not called upon to find some reference. There is practically no limit to the obscurity or seeming absurdity of certain requests—an article in the ninth edition of *Encyclopedia Britannica* (and only the ninth will do) or the minutes of a meeting of an ornithological society published in a German newspaper in 1890. Such arcana are routine for them, and it is rare indeed when they are unable to locate and borrow the needed item or have it copied if it is not to be found in the Smithsonian Libraries.

Visiting scientists and colleagues are usually astounded by, and envious of, the library resources we have at the Smithsonian, such that researchers may obtain virtually any reference with comparative ease. And it is our dedicated and often overtaxed librarians who make so much so readily accessible. They are servants of the finest caliber. Not like the inherited family servants that one of V. S. Naipaul's protagonists characterized as "limpets," but servants out of the Wodehousian mold, working intelligently behind the scenes to insure a proper outcome despite the manifest idiosyncrasies of those whom they serve.

If books are more than just words and paper, our library is surely much more than books and shelves (and now computers, which have revolutionized the operation of a library). Consider the explorers, collectors, scientists, and others responsible for gathering and presenting knowledge;

An illustration of *Grallina bruijni*, from vol. 3 of John Gould, *The Birds of New Guinea and the Adjacent Papuan Islands*, 1875–88.

the manufacturers of ink and paper, the printers, binders, publishers, editors, and even mail carriers if you will, who produce and deliver books and their components; our donors and taxpayers who make the accumulation of books possible; the preservers, arrangers, and finders of books—our librarians; and finally, the users of books who make the whole enterprise relevant and then create more knowledge and set the whole process in motion once again. Only the end of civilization will break the cycle. And civilization will not end as long as there are books and someone to read them.

Storrs L. Olson is Senior Curator of the Division of Birds, National Museum of Natural History, Smithsonian Institution.

Facing page:
Regiomontanus, *Kalendarium*
(Calendar book), 1499.

De aureo numero.

Ureum numerũ cuiuſuis ãni ſic inuenies Uide.
quotus ſit annus propoſitus a primo anno xp̃i
domini: quem numerum ſi offendes in tabula
hic appoſita aureus numerus eſt. 13. Si nõ nu
mero,primo minori illic expreſſo da. 13.ſequẽti
14 ⁊ iterum ſuccedenti. 15.ſicꝗ deinceps donec
perduceris ad numerum anni propoſiti:hoc eſt:ſingulis annis
ſingulos aureos numeros accõmoda incipiendo ab anno qui apparet in tabel
la et a. 13.primo ſcꝫ in ſerie aurei numeri ſubſcripta.Nam vbi annus tuus ſedẽ
inueniet illic habebis aureũ numerum queſitum.Sub quo etiam continuo cla
uis feſtorum mobilium cãmunisapparebit.

| 1475 |
| 1494 |
| 1513 |
| 1532 |
| 1551 |
| 1570 |

13	14	15	16	17	18	19	1	2	3	4	5	6	7	8	9	10	11	12
14	33	22	11	30	19	38	26	15	35	23	12	31	20	39	28	17	36	25

De cyclo ſolari et littera dom̃icali.

Umerus cycli ſolaris ſimili cõputo deprehenditur
per ſuam tabellam hic poſitam . Nam ſi numerus
anni ppoſiti ſcript⁹ eſt in ea tabella:cycli ſolaris nu
merus eſt. 28. Si non eſt iliic expreſſus:da proxio
minori ibidem ſcripto.28.ſequenti. 1.ac rurſus ſuc
cedenti.2.ſicꝗ deinceps queãdmodũ de aureo nu
mero precipiebatur donec ad annũ ppoſitum peruenies .Nam vbi talis anno
rum ſuppuratio deſinet:illic in ſerie cycli ſolaris ſub ſcripta numerum cycli ſola
ris queſitum agnoſces Sub eo autem numero cycli ſolariscõtinuo habebis lit
teram dñicalem anni tui:que ſi vnica occurrat:annũ eſſe cõmunem intelliges:ſi
dupler biſſextilem. Prior ideſt ſuperior ad feſtũ vſcꝗ mathie apoſtoli vtilis erit
Inferior autem ad reliquam anni partem accõmodabitur.

| 1475 |
| 1503 |
| 1531 |
| 1559 |
| 1587 |
| 1615 |

28	1	2	3	4	5	6	7	8	9	10	11	12	13	14	15	16	17	18	19	20	21	22	23	24	25	26	27
A	g	e	d	c	b	g	f	e	d	b	H	g	f	d	c	b	H	f	e	d	c	H	g	f	e	c	b
f			A			c				e				g			b				D						

De inditione.

Porro vt breuiter res vulgatas percurramus haud
diſſimiliter colligetur numerus cycli inditionalis
aſſumpta preſenti tabella ãnor chriſti domini quo
rum vnuſquiſcꝗ habet.8.ideſt cycli inditionalis oc
tauus eſt. Ceteri autem anni in tabella non appa
rentes ſm̃ juditionis ſerie hic ſubiunctam diſtributi ſuos quincꝗ
numeros inuenient.

| 1475 |
| 1490 |
| 1505 |
| 1520 |
| 1525 |

8	9	10	11	12	13	14	15	1	2	3	4	5	6	7

Introduction

Throughout time, voyagers and explorers have drawn readers with them to unknown lands through their stories, captured in song and legend, early manuscripts, and printed books. Intriguing those who stayed at home, each report broadened the horizons of readers, who understood their world differently as they learned about faraway places. This exhibition is such a voyage, an invitation to travel through lesser-known Smithsonian collections, to share important books in the Smithsonian Libraries, and to learn about the working life of the Smithsonian Institution.

For 155 years, as its researchers have explored and gathered materials from around the world, the Smithsonian Institution has curated and protected scientific and artistic discoveries. Since 1846 the Smithsonian has collected and maintained a widely diverse body of objects that reflect the nation's intellectual awakening and a growing interest in exploring and understanding the universe. These activities fulfill the mandate of the Smithsonian's founder, James Smithson, an English gentleman-scientist. For reasons that have never been known, Smithson in 1826 willed his estate to the United States, which he had never visited, "to found at Washington, under the name of the Smithsonian Institution, an Establishment for the increase and diffusion of knowledge." Through its research,

study, analysis, and interpretation (the "increase"), and through its publications, exhibitions, and educational programs (the "diffusion"), the Smithsonian contributes substantially to our nation's cultural and scientific heritage. Smithsonian scholars engage in individual journeys of discovery each time they examine artifacts or consult the written and illustrated records of voyages undertaken by earlier generations. By building on accumulated wisdom, they extend their journeys even further.

Bolstering and complementing the Smithsonian collections is a library system that meets the needs of staff and public alike. Books and manuscripts provide a strong foundation for all enterprises of the Institution and for outside scholars and visitors. The Smithsonian Libraries acquires books because scientists, curators, education specialists, and designers refer to primary sources daily, for inspiration and information. The Libraries has become a treasure house of rare books, manuscripts, and artifacts. Materials once collected for research and display grow more valuable with age, and in preserving them, the Smithsonian Libraries preserves for the country another part of its rich heritage.

Voyages of discovery can be of many kinds: a journey to an unknown place, a mental exploration of familiar territory, a rediscovery of an earlier age, or a wholly new episode of creative thought. Join

us for an expedition in three phases. First, visit the world as Europeans knew and recorded it in early printed texts, and follow as their curiosity drove them beyond their borders. Their stories of what they found compelled others to pursue the unknown. As societies developed new and better navigational tools, explorers ventured farther. With each new voyage and its discoveries, the European worldview expanded. Writers, artists, and printers collaborated to document all that was new, producing lavishly illustrated reports of peoples, animals, plants, and lands.

Second, join explorers in science to probe vistas of the intellect. By reasoning and through experimentation, scientists have extended our understanding of the world to the heavens above and the earth below. Sometimes their speculations led to actual voyages, but more often they sought a result or outcome, reached through experimentation and the scientific method.

The leaders of our third voyage are artists and writers, explorers of the imagination. Writers and other creative thinkers advance into new territory, proposing and solving questions that stimulate consideration by others. Words and paper challenge artists to present these visions in two-dimensional media. Finding ways to achieve this has resulted in items of great beauty and permanence. The Smithsonian Libraries is the guardian of this accumulated knowledge. We invite you to come with us on a journey of discovery.

Detail from ANDRÉ VERA, *Le nouveau jardin* (The new garden), 1912.

I. Journeys over Land and Sea

The Smithsonian Libraries collection of travel voyages documents the ever-expanding worldview of humankind. In every age, pioneers pushed beyond their own boundaries to chart new lands and observe exotic plants, animals, and peoples. Among the earliest works in the Smithsonian collection are maps, republished in the Renaissance, that were prepared for the Greek and Roman geographers/historians Ptolemy and Pliny. Often copied from manuscripts or gathered from travelers' stories, such star charts, bestiaries, and herbals contain pictures and descriptions that give scholars evidence about life in earlier centuries. Olaus Magnus, a Swedish bishop who traveled widely in Scandinavia and Europe during the mid-sixteenth century, compiled the first major work on the peoples, geography, economy, and fauna of northern Europe. In 1483 Bernhard von Breydenbach made a pilgrimage to Jerusalem, and his account is enlivened by the first use of colorful panoramas. Both books express the anxieties of the earliest travelers, who journeyed into the unknown fearful of monsters, savage weather, and plummeting over the edge of the world.

As their curiosity and bravery grew, people sailed farther with the aid of specialized instruments. With more accurate astronomical tables and tools, navigators could leave the coastline for the open ocean and steer by the stars. Refinements in navigation would lead to the discovery of new continents. Artists, observers, writers, and printers recorded and depicted all that was learned about the expanding world. Through direct observation, the quality and accuracy of illustrations and descriptions of rare animals and plants vastly improved, as shown by printed works of great beauty.

Although nations undertook the great voyages of exploration primarily to expand their territories, scientific and artistic discoveries abounded. Voyagers returned with specimens from the natural world as well as ideas that enriched and changed life. To obtain a deeper understanding of them, scholars cataloged and organized their findings in works such as Pierre Belon's *Observations* (1553).

By the early seventeenth century, learned societies and mercantile groups launched highly organized expeditions solely for scientific and commercial purposes. Scientists and artists were integral partners in these expeditions, and the specimens they collected and recorded are now housed in natural history museums around the world. The medieval cabinet of curiosities acquired a scientific character as plants, animals, and minerals flowed back to Europe from foreign regions.

The illustrated book reached its apogee in lavishly colored and engraved volumes produced by travelers and illustrators. Their work forms an important body of literature of unparalleled value to historians, ecologists, scientists, and many others.

Detail of "Atsina Camp," from vol. 5 of EDWARD S. CURTIS, *The North American Indian*, 1909.

Travelers and Places

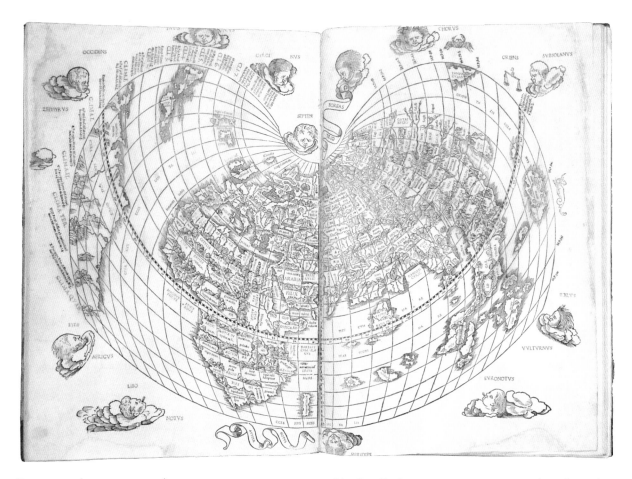

Ptolemy (ca. 100–170)
Liber geographiae (Book of geography).
[Venice: Iacobum Pentium de Leucho, 1511].
Gift of the Burndy Library.

Claudius Ptolemaeus, an astronomer and mathematician living in Alexandria, Egypt, summed up the geography of the known world—essentially the Roman Empire—in the second century A.D. He systematically listed the latitudes and longitudes of some eight thousand places in Europe, Africa, and Asia, and he described methods of projection for drawing maps. Representing a major advance in the science of mapmaking, despite its errors, Ptolemy's work retained its authority for almost 1,400 years. It survived for centuries through manuscript copying and was put into print in 1475, all the while expanding as geographical knowledge increased. The 1511 edition is the first to include a bit of North America in the world map.

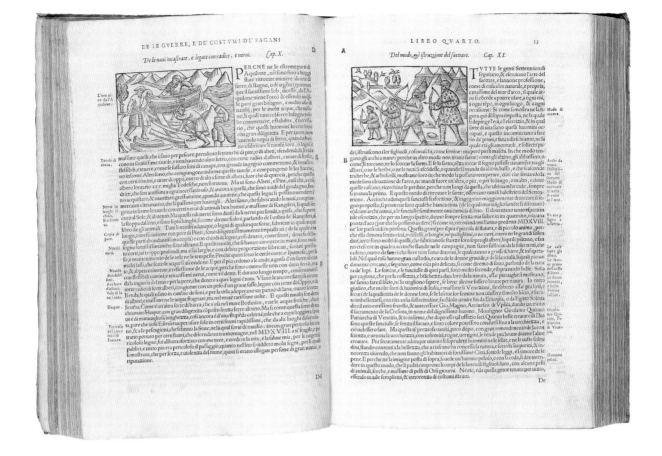

detail

Olaus Magnus (1490–1557)

Historia delle genti et della natura delle cose settentrionali
(History of the northern peoples and things of nature).
Venice: Giunti, 1565. Gift of the Burndy Library.

Olaus Magnus intended his work, first published in
Latin (Rome, 1555), to be an explication of his great
map of the lands of the north, which he created in 1539.
Woodcuts show northern peoples, including Lapps and
Finns, engaged in their daily occupations, which were
no doubt exotic and strange to southern Europeans.
The volume includes some of the first illustrations of
whaling, and readers may have readily accepted as real
the various fantastical monsters depicted throughout
the popular and widely translated book.

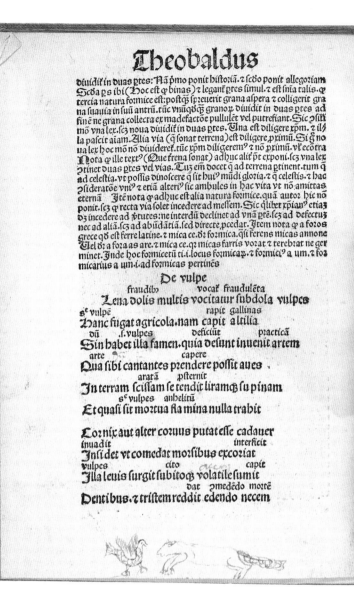

diuidit in duas ptes: Ãã pmo ponit histoziã. z scðo ponit allegoziam
Scða ps ibi (Hoc est q̃ binas) z leganf ptes simul. z est snia talis. q̃
tercia natura formice est: postq̃ spreuerit grana aspera z colligerit gra
na suauia in suũ antrũ. tũc vnũqðq̃ granoz diuidit in duas ptes ad
fine ne grana collecta ex madefactõe pullulet vel putrefiant. Sic ᵱsiti
mõ vna lex. scz noua diuidit in duas ptes. Vna est diligere xpm. z il/
la pascit aiam. Alia via (q̃ sonat terrena) est diligere ᵱ primũ. Si g̃ no
ua lex hoc mõ nõ diuideref. tũc xpm diligerem⁹ z nõ primũ. vl'ecõtra
Nota q̃ ille text⁹ (Que frena sonat) adhuc alif ᵱt exponi. scz vna lex
ᵱtinet duas ptes vel vias. Tuz em docet q̃ ad terrena ᵱtinent. tum q̃
ad celestia. vt possis dinoscere q̃ sit hui⁹ mũdi gloria. z q̃ celestis. z hac
ᵱsideratõe vni⁹ z etiã alteri⁹ sic ambules in hac vita vt nõ amittas
eternã   Ité nota q̃ adhuc est alia natura formice. quã autoz hic nõ
ponit. scz q̃ recta via solet incedere ad messem. Sic q̃libet xpian⁹ etiaz
dz incedere ad ᵱtutes: ne interdũ declinet ad vnã ᵱte. scz ad defectuz
nec ad aliã. scz ad abũdãtia. sed directe. pcedat. Item nota q̃ a foros
grece qð est ferre latine. z mica ce. ðz formica. q̃ si ferens micas annone
Vel ðz a foza as are. z mica ce. qz micas farris vozat z terebzat ne ger
minet. Inde hoc formicetũ ti. i. locus formicaz. z formici⁹ a um. z foz
micarius a um. i. ad formicas pertinés

De vulpe

fraudib⁹   vocaf frauduléta
Lena dolis multis vocitatur subdola vulpes
s^e vulpé   rapit gallinas
Hanc fugat agricola. nam capit a liilia
   dũ .s. vulpes   deficiũt   practicã
Sin habet illa famen. quia desunt inuenit artem
   arte   capere
Qua sibi cantantes prendere possit aues
         ararã   psternit
In terram scissam se tendit liramq̃ su pinam
      s^e vulpes   anhelitũ
Et quasi sit moztua fla mina nulla trahit

Cozniz aut alter cozuus putat esse cadauer
inuadit   interficit
Insidet vt comedat mozsibus excoziat
vulpes   cito   capit
Illa leuis surgit subitoq̃ volatile sumit
               dat ᵱmedédo mozte
Dentibus. z tristem reddit edendo necem

Theobaldus Episcopus
Phisiologus . . . de naturis duodecim animalium
(On the nature of animals) with drawings of animals.
[Cologne]: Henricus Quentell, [1494]. Gift of the
Burndy Library.

Fantastical monsters were a common feature of
medieval bestiaries, which derived from classical texts
of the second to fourth centuries A.D. The bestiary
incorporated oral traditions, travelers' tales, Christian
symbolism, and allegory into a compendium of moral-
izing tales based on animals familiar, exotic, and sometimes imaginary. Copied and recopied in manuscript
form over a thousand years, these texts became more
varied and elaborate when printed versions proliferated
in the late 1400s. The genre as a whole, however, was
soon superseded by the more scientific works of the
Renaissance.

[*Gart der Gesundheit*] (The garden of health). [Ulm?:
Konrad Dinckmut?, 1487?]. Gift of E. R. Squibb &
Sons and Bristol-Myers Squibb Co.

Gart der Gesundheit is one of the earliest printed ver-
nacular works in the medieval herbal tradition. Herbals
combined folklore and home remedies, information
from classical sources, and religious symbolism into a
popular mix of botanical and medical advice. With text
and woodcut images often copied from earlier works,
rather than drawn from nature, herbals became increasingly corrupted and stereotyped over time. While some
illustrations remain identifiable, even charming to the
modern eye, others are unrecognizable, frustrating both
contemporaries and modern researchers.

Euforbiū gemischet mit baum
öle vnd die wassersüchtigen geli-
der domit geschmieret hilffet sere·
Difes auff die lebern vnd milcz
geschmieret benimet den schmercze
donon· Euforbium in die nasen
gelassen machet fast nyesen/ vnd
zeubet vil böser feuchtung auß dē
haubt· Euforbiū gemischet mit
oleo de spica vnnd die stirn domit
bestrichen vnd oben auf dē haubt
benymet die geschwere auß dem
haubt genāt litargia frenesis/ vñ
machet gūt sisi/ vnd benimet auch
also gestriche an den halß squinan
ciam das ist ain geschwere in dem
halß· Auch spricht Johānes me
sue das euforbium behalten mūg
werden·xl·iar/vñ ist alt besser dañ
frisch/ wann so es ye frischer ist so
ist es mer gifftig dann so es alt ist
vnd das merck dobey das man dē
gūmi nit genahen darff so es auß
dem baum fleußt als oben stat·

Gebrent ercz
Das clxxi Capitel

Es vstū latine·grece calc9
vel calcutecaumienan vel
culcostaumenan·· Die
maister sprechen das diß seie haiß
vnd trucken an dem vierden grade
Difes rainiget melancoliaz/ vñ
darūn machet man es in die pfla
ster die do dienen dem milczen dar
auß dann entspringet melancolei·
Es vstū erczt auß faul flaisch·/
Es vstum gemischet mit hönig

vnd mit saiffen/ vnd dises gelasse
in ain fistel hailt sie zeh and· We
licher den gebresten het genant po
lipus dz ist ain flaisch wachset in
der nasen der neme es vstum vnnd
sirewe es auf ain pflaster genant
axicroceon/od auf ain apostolicū
vnd lege das darauff es erzet dz
ab vnd hailet es on zweifel·

Elephanten zan
Das clxxii Capitel

Bur latine Die maister
sprechent das ebur haisse
ains elephanten zan/dar
umb ist des elephanten figur hye
gesetzet vmb seines gelides willen
dz gar in manger erznei genützt
wirt/auch gar grosse tuget darīn
erfunden ist· Von disem zan ge
schabet buluer vnd das gemischt

n j

C. PLINII
SECVNDI NATVRALIS
HISTORIAE LIBER
SECVNDVS.

An sit mundus, & an vnus. CAP. I.

MVNDVM † & hoc, quod nomine alio cœlum appellare libuit, cuius circunflexu teguntur cuncta, numen esse credi par est, æternum, immensum, neq; genitum, neq; interiturum vnquam. Huius extera indagare, nec interest hominum, nec capit humanæ coniectúra mentis. Sacer est, æternus, immensus, totus in toto, imò verò ipse totum: finitus, & infinito similis: omnium rerum certus, & similis incerto: extrà, intrà, cuncta complexus in se, idemq́; rerum naturæ opus, & rerū ipsa natura. Furor est, mensuram eius animo quosdam agitasse, atq; prodere ausos: alios rursus occasione hinc sumpta, aut his data, innumerabiles tradidisse mūdos, vt totidem rerū naturas credi oporteret: aut, si vna omnes incubaret, totidem tamen Soles, totidémque Lunas, & cætera etiam in vno & immensa, & innumerabilia sidera: quasi non eadem quæstione semper in termino cogitationis occursura, desiderio finis alicuius: aut, si hæc infinitas naturæ omnium artifici possit assignari, non illud idem in vno faciliùs sit intelligi, tanto præsertim opere. Furor est, profectò furor, egredi ex eo: & tanquam interna eius cuncta planè iam sint nota, ita scrutari extera: quasi verò mensuram vllius rei possit agere, qui sui nesciat: aut mens hominis videre, quæ mundus ipse non capiat.

† *Aliàs sic, & hoc, quodcunque cœlū appellare libuit.*

De forma eius. CAP. II.

FOrmam eius in speciem orbis absoluti globatam esse, nomen in primis & consensus in eo mortalium, orbem appellantium, sed & argumenta rerum docent: non solùm quia talis figura omnibus sui partibus vergit in sese, ac sibi ipsa toleranda est, séque includit & continet, nullarū egens compaginum, nec finem aut initium vllis sui partibus sentiens, nec quia ad motum, † quo subinde verti debeat (vt mox apparebit) talis aptissima est: sed oculorum quoque probatione, quòd conuexus mediusque quacunque cernatur, quum id accidere in alia non possit figura.

† *quo subinde vert.i mox apparebit.*

De motu eius. CAP. III.

HAnc ergo formam eius, æterno & irrequieto ambitu inenarrabili celeritate, vigintiquatuor horarum spatio circumagi, Solis exortus & occasus haud dubiū reliquére. An sit immensus, & ideò sensum aurium facilè excedens, tantæ molis rotatæ vertigine assidua sonitus, non equidem facilè dixerim, non hercle magis, quàm circumactorum simul tinnitus siderum, suosque voluentium orbes: an dulci quidem & incredibili suauitate concentus, nobis qui intus agimus, iuxta diebus noctibusq́; tacitus labitur mundus. Esse innumeras ei effigies animalium rerumq́; cunctarum impressas, nec (vt in volucrum notamus ouis) læuitate continua lubricum corpus, quod clarissimi

A authores

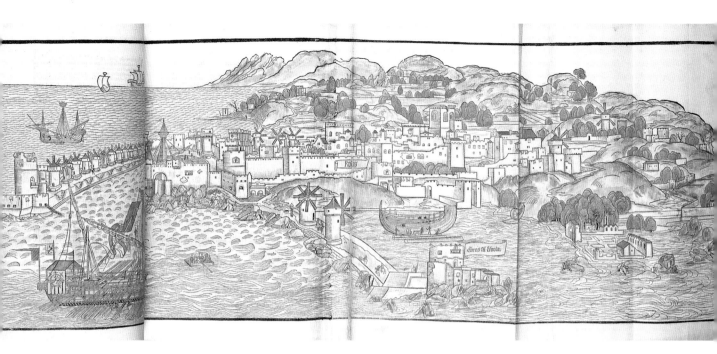

Bernhard von Breydenbach (d. 1497)

Peregrinatio in terram sanctam (Travel to the Holy Land). Mainz: Erhard Reuwich, 1486. Gift of the Burndy Library.

Breydenbach's account of his 1483 pilgrimage to the Holy Land is thought to be the first printed travel book. Fellow traveler Erhard Reuwich, the first painter known to have published a book, created its fine hand-colored woodcuts. His illustrations include the first use of panoramas to depict cities encountered along the way, such as the view of Rhodes seen above. Panoramas, enlivened by great detail, became a popular illustrative form in early printed books.

left

Pliny the Elder (ca. 23–79)

Naturalis historia (Natural history). Frankfurt: Martin Lechler, 1582. Gift of the Burndy Library.

Naturalis historia is the most thorough zoological and botanical treatise known from the ancient world. Gaius Plinius Secundus, a well-traveled military officer of the Roman Empire and a historian, deliberately attempted to record all knowledge of the world and nature, preserving that written by earlier authors and adding to it from his direct experiences. A man of intense curiosity, he died after venturing too close to the erupting Mount Vesuvius. The 1582 edition, with woodcuts by artists Jost Amman and Hans Weidlitz, is one of the few illustrated versions among the fifteen editions (published from 1469 to 1800) that are held in the Smithsonian Libraries.

6 4
2

5
7 5
9 9
5345

Tabula ad Lōgitudinē logiorē			Eclipsis ad lōgitudinē ppiorē						Tabella de Coloribꝰ Eclipsiū Solis
Latitudo Lune viſa	Důcta	ūiſinuta caſus	Latitudo Lune viſa	Důcta	ūiſinuta caſus				
ṁ ʒ	p	ṁ ʒ	ṁ ʒ	p	ṁ ʒ				☉ Logitudinis
31 0	0	0 0	34 0	0	13 0				A Modo
28 18	1	12 39	31 18	1	13 16			1	Nigrū preſſum
25 35	2	17 30	28 35	2	18 25			2	Nigrū obſcurū
22 52	3	20 25	25 53	3	22 2			3	Fuſcū in rubore
20 17	4	23 33	23 10	4	24 50			4	Fuſcū in croceo
17 18	5	25 36	20 20	5	27 9			5	Fuſcum larum
14 41	6	27 36	17 45	6	29 0			6	Fuſcū rubeum
11 3	7	28 34	15 3	7	30 30			7	Ruſſum
9 20	8	29 33	11 10	8	31 56			8	Ruſſum
6 38	9	30 17	9 38	9	32 37			9	Rubeū glaucū
3 55	10	30 45	6 55	10	33 16			10	Rubeū glaucū
1 3	11	30 59	4 13	11	33 44			11	Croceum
0 0	12	31 0	1 30	12	33 48			12	Croceū album
			0 0	12	34 0				

Pars duodecima puncti equalis ad Solem ꝫ Lunam			Tabula ꝗntitatis tenebraꝛū in ytraꝗ Eclipſi.				
Puncta	Diametri.	ad Solem	ad Lunam	Puncta	Diametri.	ad Solem	ad Lunam
	☉	☽		☽			Tabella de coloribꝰ Eclipſiū Lune.
	p ṁ	p ṁ		p ṁ	p ṁ		☉ Longitudinis
1	0 20	0 30	1	0 20	0 30	10	Nigrū preſſum
2	1 0	1 10	2	1 0	1 10		
3	1 45	2 8	3	1 50	2 5	10	Nigrū cū viridi
4	2 40	3 10	4	2 40	3 10		(tate ꝫ aureo.
5	3 40	4 20	5	3 20	4 10	30	Nigrū ſubaubē
6	4 40	5 30	6	4 40	5 30	40	Glaucū cum
7	5 50	6 45	7	5 50	6 40		(pallore
8	7 0	8 0	8	7 0	8 0	50	Pallida ꝫ griſea
9	8 20	9 10	9	8 20	9 10	60	Griſea cum al
10	9 40	10 20	10	9 40	10 20		(bedine.
11	10 50	11 20	11	10 50	11 20		
12	12 0	12 0	12	12 0	12 0	90	Ruſſum

ALFONSO X, KING OF CASTILE AND LEON (1221–1284)

Tabule astronomice (Astronomical tables). Venice: Johannes Hamman, 1492. Gift of the Burndy Library.

Navigators for Columbus would have taken the Alfonsine tables, a set of astronomical tables, on their expeditions to the New World. Once thought to have been devised by astronomers at the court of Alfonso X, the tables were extremely useful to navigators and crucial to early explorers. Because the tables considerably simplified astronomical calculations, the user could determine planetary positions without having to work with the underlying mathematical models that described the Ptolemaic solar system.

right

JAMES BASSANTIN (1504?–1568)

Astronomia (Astronomy). [Lyon]: Jean de Tournes, 1599. Gift of the Burndy Library.

Volvelles, printed paper instruments, provided astronomers with the positions of the Sun, Moon, and planets without having to resort to lengthy calculations derived from planetary tables. Bassantin's work, a general overview of astronomy, partly copies Petrus Apianus's *Astronomicum Cæsareum* of 1540. The Irish astronomer William Molyneux (1656–1698) once owned this copy.

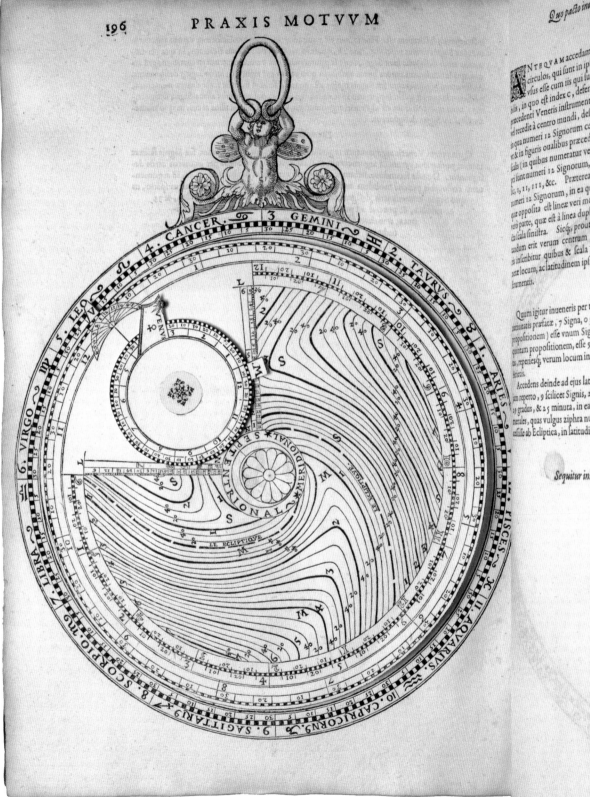

WILLIAM GILBERT (1540–1603)

De magnete, magneticisque corporibus, et de magno magnete tellure . . . (On the magnet, magnetic bodies, and the great magnet of the earth). London: P. Short, 1600. Gift of the Burndy Library.

Although the magnetic lodestone had been used since ancient Greek times, Gilbert's work contains the first experimental research on the properties of magnetism. Gilbert argued correctly that the Earth was a natural magnet, and the Earth's magnetic poles are relatively near the geographic poles. As a result, mariners were better able to use the lodestone as an effective navigational tool.

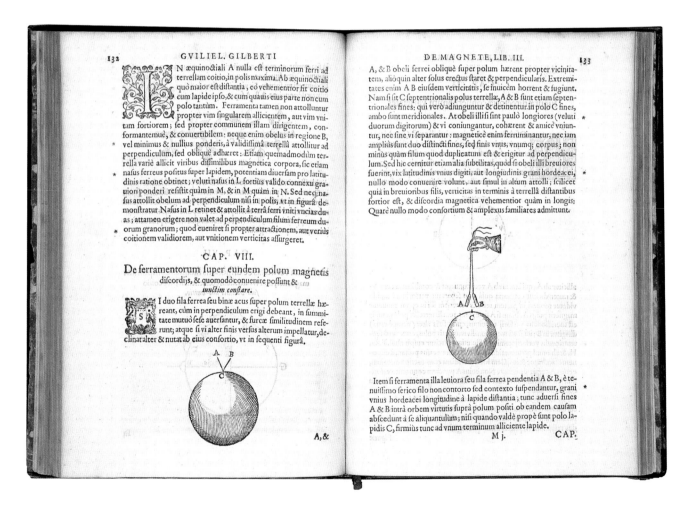

Journeys over Land and Sea

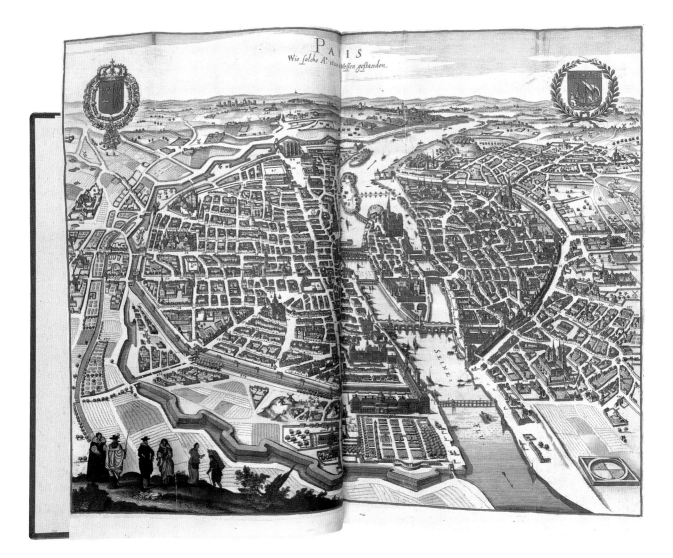

MARTIN ZEILLER (1589–1661)
Topographia Galliae (Topography of Gaul).
Frankfurt: Caspar Merian, 1655–61. 4 vols.
Mary Stuart Book Fund.

Zeiller, an Austrian cartographer, dedicated this four-volume survey of the provinces and towns of France to its king, Louis XIV. (It was part of a much more extensive geographic survey of many European countries.) The volume containing his three hundred illustrations is one of the period's finest examples of hand-colored engraving. The finely rendered pictures preserve many details of buildings, roadways, and cities that no longer exist or have been significantly altered. *Topographia* is an excellent example of the art of the book in seventeenth-century France and one of the most comprehensive contemporary guides to its cities and structures.

EXPERIMENTUM I.

MODUS VI.

EXPERIMENTUM II.

MODUS VII.

EXPERIMENTUM.

---

above and right

ATHANASIUS KIRCHER (1602–1680)

Mundus subterraneus (Underground world).
Amsterdam: Joannem Janssonium and Elizeum
Weyerstraten, 1664–65.

An intensely inquisitive man, the Jesuit polymath Athanasius Kircher pursued research in the fields of geography, language, astronomy, mathematics, and medicine. He authored more than forty books, including *Mundus subterraneus*, perhaps the earliest printed work on geophysics and volcanology. Recent earthquakes and the 1630 eruption of Mount Vesuvius prompted Kircher's interest. To satisfy his curiosity, he climbed Vesuvius and was lowered by rope into the crater. In his book he speculated on the nature of phenomena that occur below the Earth's surface, and explained and illustrated the origins of fossils, hot springs, and volcanoes.

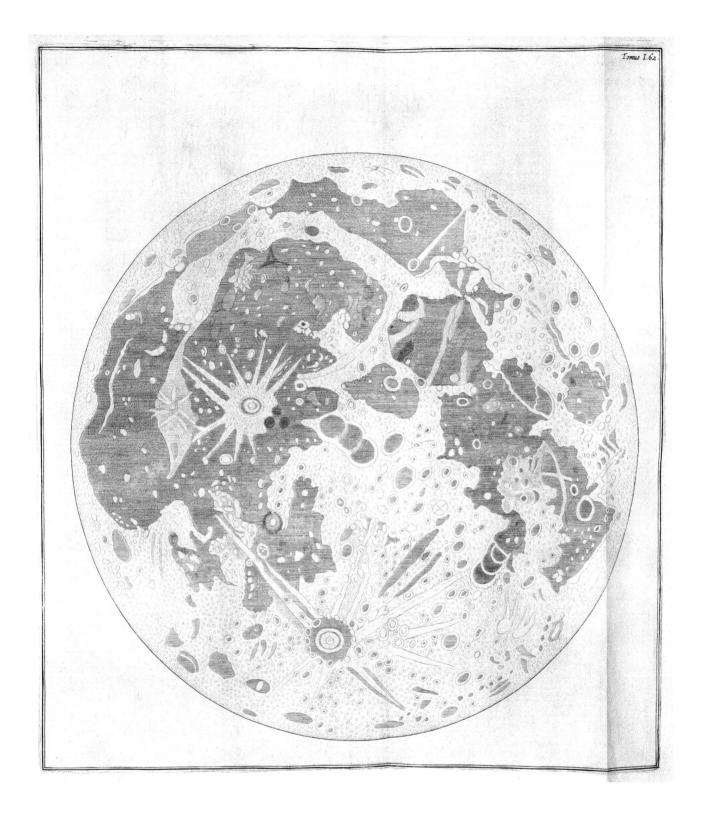

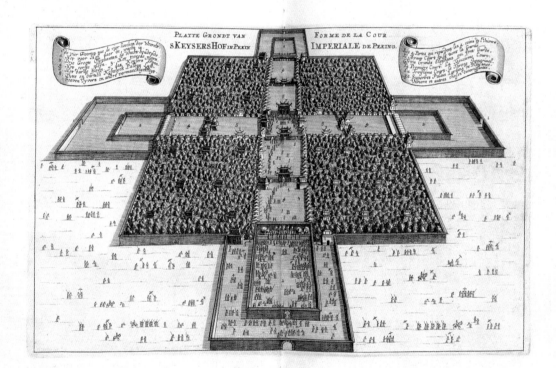

Levin Vincent (1658–1727)

Elenchus tabularum . . . , in gazophylacio Levini Vincent
(A series of illustrations . . . of Levin Vincent's collection of the marvels of nature). Haarlem: Sumptibus Auctoris, 1719.

Reflecting the spirit of exploration and inquiry that began to emerge in Europe in the late sixteenth century, individuals of means took to assembling collections of curiosities. Some served as aids in classifying all known plants and animals. Among its varied holdings, the natural history collection of Dutch merchant Levin Vincent contained animals preserved in alcohol, skeletons and skins, and plants dried and pressed on paper. These same items, as well as books, remain the core materials of taxonomy and systematics, fields of research that continue today at the Smithsonian.

left

Johannes Nieuhof (1618–1672)

Het gezantschap . . . aan den grooten Tartarischen Cham, den tegenwoordigen keizer van China (An embassy . . . to the Grand Tartar Cham, emperor of China). Amsterdam: by Jacob van Meurs, 1665. Mary Stuart Book Fund.

This remarkable travel account by an agent of the Dutch East India Company details the culture, landscape, peoples, architecture, festivals, and cities of seventeenth-century China. During the age of Western exploration and imperialism in the Far East, Europeans craved information on exotic lands, and this book profoundly affected them. Designers copied its illustrations of Chinese ornament and used them as inspiration for creating decorative objects and furniture.

MARK CATESBY (1682–1749)
The Natural History of Carolina, Florida and the Bahama Islands. London: for the author, 1731–43 [1729–48]. 2 vols. Gift of Marcia Brady Tucker.

Even among the many beautifully illustrated works in natural history in the Smithsonian Libraries, the two-volume magnum opus of Mark Catesby is extraordinary. The work is the product of one man's dedication and effort, from his years of travel and research to his hand-coloring of the printed plates (which he learned to etch himself so as to implement his own technique for indicating feathers). Linnaeus cited more than a hundred of his species descriptions, and the book is the first fully illustrated work on the flora and fauna of southeastern North America. Plants and animals often are grouped in their natural associations, and the folio format allowed many species to be depicted life size. The Smithsonian Libraries holds a magnificent copy of the first edition, complete with the rare prospectus and the advertisement for the Appendix, in a contemporary full-leather binding. Formerly owned by Marcia Brady Tucker and Evan Morton Evans, the book has a distinguished provenance that traces back to the Abdy family, noted for its support of natural history publications in eighteenth-century England.

JAMES COOK (1728–1779)
A Voyage towards the South Pole, and round the World performed in His Majesty's ships the Revolution *and* Adventure *in the years 1772, 1773, 1774, and 1775.*
2 vols. London: W. Strahan and T. Cadell, 1777.

James Cook's voyages initiated the modern era of scientific exploration. Establishing a model for future expeditions, his three voyages had an explicitly scientific rather than political purpose, carrying artists and naturalists who brought back large collections of plants, animals, and ethnographic artifacts from the regions visited. In his second voyage (1772–75), considered by many the most remarkable voyage ever, Cook circumnavigated the world at the Antarctic Circle with the benefit of a new instrument, the chronometer, which enabled him to determine the ship's longitude accurately.

Coleoptera.
1
Buprestis ignita

Hemiptera.
2
Cimex

Hymenoptera.
5
Tenthredo

Lepidoptera
3
Papilio Antiopa

Mᵒ Harris del et Sc

The
NATURALIST'S,
and
TRAVELLER'S COMPANION,
Containing
Instructions for collecting & Preserving Objects of
NATURAL HISTORY,
and
for promoting inquiries after Human
Knowledge in General.
the Second Edition corrected & Enlarged
BY John Coakley Lettfom M·D·F·R·S·& S·A.

Neuroptera.
4
Panorpa coa.

Diptera.
6
Musca.

Aptera.
7
Aranea.

LONDON: Printed for E. & C. Dilly, 1774.

JOHN COAKLEY LETTSOM (1744–1815)

The Naturalist's and Traveller's Companion, containing Instructions for Collecting & Preserving Objects of Natural History. 2nd ed. London: E. & C. Dilly, 1774. Charles W. Richmond Collection.

Battling careless handling, rot, bugs, and inadvertent damage, European scientists and collectors exercised considerable ingenuity in getting specimens safely back home for study and in keeping them safe once there. In 1772 Lettsom, a British physician who had a private natural-history museum and botanical garden, produced one of the earliest and most handsome manuals on collecting, preparing, transporting, and preserving scientific specimens. Charles W. Richmond, a Smithsonian ornithologist and bibliographer, acquired this book in the early twentieth century. Smithsonian staff have always collected and donated books to the Institution, and as a result, its library collections document museum practices from the 1600s into the present century.

CHARLES WILKES (1798–1877)

Narrative of the United States Exploring Expedition . . . 5 vols. and atlas. Philadelphia: Lea and Blanchard, 1845.

By the 1830s, the United States determined to assert itself in the economic and scientific exploration of the Pacific, including the western coast of North America. Lt. Charles Wilkes, U.S. Navy, led the first official scientific expedition to the region in 1838. Navigators and hydrographers, along with scientists, naturalists, and artists, explored areas from Alaska to Antarctica for five years. The materials they collected are preserved at the Smithsonian's National Museum of Natural History and are still invaluable for the study of the peoples, animals, plants, and geography of the eastern Pacific.

TITIAN RAMSAY PEALE (1799–1885)

Mammalia and Ornithology. Philadelphia: printed by C. Sherman, 1848.

Peale, the youngest son of American artist Charles Willson Peale, was one of the naturalists appointed to the United States Exploring Expedition of 1838–42. Peale's report is extremely scarce; official distribution was limited to an initial seventy copies. Because Charles Wilkes, the expedition's leader, suppressed parts of the report and other naturalists criticized the accuracy of his nomenclature, Wilkes arranged for a new report, prepared by John Cassin in 1858. Cassin quoted Peale's field observations at length and included an atlas of Peale's and other plates. The Smithsonian Libraries holds two copies of Peale's complete and extremely rare work, both in their original bindings.

106   ZOOLOGY.

The form and general aspect of this bird is more that of the Raven than of the Crow; the bill is arched like that of the Raven, and the tail is of the same form, but the acutely pointed quills, and short nails, particularly those on the outer toes, present a marked character, which separates it from any other which we have had an opportunity to examine.

The specimen from which our description is taken, was shot within a short distance of the City of Funchal, on the Island of Madeira, in the month of September. They were not uncommon, but we were not so fortunate as to obtain a male, not suspecting at the time, that it was an undescribed species.

CORVUS HAWAIIENSIS.—(Nob.)

PLATE XXVIII.

Alala of the Hawaiians.

C. formâ similis C. coraci ; colore vix non penitùs fuliginoso-brunneo, remigibus nonnihil pallidioribus : corporis totius plumis ad basin plumbeis : rostro, tibiis unguibusque cærulescenti-nigris : iride brunneâ : plumulis setaceis nares contegentibus nigris irescentibusque : remigum tribus primis gradatis, quartâ longissimâ ; scapis suprà nigris, subtùs albis : caudâ rotundatâ, ex duodecim conflatâ plumis ; scapis supernè nigris, subtùs fuliginosis.

In form like the Raven; colour nearly uniform, sooty brown; the quills somewhat lighter; all the feathers of the body lead-coloured at the roots; bill, legs, and claws, blue-black; irides brown; setaceous feathers, covering the nostrils, black and glossy; three first quills graduated, fourth longer; shafts black above, white beneath; tail rounded, consisting of twelve feathers; shaft black above, sooty beneath.

One specimen measures $18\frac{7}{8}$ inches total length; bill, $2\frac{4}{10}$ inches; tarsus, $2\frac{1}{2}$ inches; hind claw, $\frac{6}{10}$ inch. Male?

A second: total length, $17\frac{1}{4}$ inches; bill, 2 inches; tarsus, $2\frac{2}{10}$ inches. Female?

THE AURORA BOREALIS.

"THE heavens declare the glory of God;" (Ps. xix. i.) yet the more familiar appearances of the sky, beautiful as they are, scarcely awaken our attention, or lead our thoughts towards their Great Author. But when such a spectacle as that presented by the Aurora Borealis first breaks upon the sight, the most indifferent person must be led to reflect upon the wonder-working power of the Divine Hand.

The name given to this phenomenon signifies Northern Daybreak, and is very appropriate, because the Aurora usually appears in the north, and gives a light not unlike that of the dawn of day. It is sometimes seen in this country; but it is seldom brighter here than the light of a subdued twilight. In the regions of the north, and also at rare intervals in this country, it assumes a much more magnificent appearance, and presents a variety of majestic forms. Sometimes from a focus of light, there proceeds a multitude of bright and quivering beams, shooting upwards with great rapidity, and yielding a silvery radiance like that of the moon. Frequently a larger arch of light appears, accompanied at the same time by other smaller arches; these move towards each other, and suddenly unite in one splendid mass of radiance; or, perhaps one majestic slow-moving arch, of great beauty and effulgence, will suddenly break into countless masses of light, or into numerous smaller arches. Sometimes these arches are brightest towards their centres, at others they are most brilliant at their extremities.

The light of the Aurora is generally white and silvery, but it occasionally presents the beautiful colouring of the rainbow. In high northern latitudes it is mostly white, steel-grey, or pale yellow; but when the sky is clear, or only thin films of cloud are visible, the colours are vivid and prismatic. In Baffin's Bay, the Aurora has been observed distinctly of red, orange, yellow, and green colours. In the north-east of Siberia, it is particularly luminous, clothing the sky with a radiance resembling that of "gold, rubies, and sapphires." In Hudson's Bay the light of the Aurora is frequently equal to that of the full-moon, while in Lapland and Sweden the light is still more brilliant, and nearly constant. In this beautiful phenomenon, therefore, the inhabitants of polar regions find a compensation for many of the discomforts and inconveniences of their dreary situation. Even in the Shetland isles the Aurora is a frequent and welcome visiter. Under the title of "merry dancers," the inhabitants hail its appearance as giving beauty and cheerfulness to their long winter nights. It appears soon after the commencement of evening twilight, rising just above the horizon, without particular motion or effulgence, but after a time breaking forth into streams of brilliant light, and assuming every possible variety of form and colour; the stars are visible through the streamers of the Aurora, and they are not greatly dimmed in their lustre, unless the light is of remarkable brilliancy. Objects on the earth may also be observed through these transparent beams. A splendid Aurora was observed by Captain Parry, actually shooting its beams between the observer and the land, the latter being only three thousand yards distant.

The cause of the Aurora has never been satisfactorily explained. It is, however, usually attributed to electricity, which, in its passage from the north pole to the equator, is supposed to become visible in this form. The beautiful imitation of the streamers of the Aurora, which can be obtained from the electrical machine, seems to favour this view; yet it is remarkable that the magnetic needle has never been visibly affected by the Aurora even in those countries where the phenomenon is the most splendid. This is still, therefore, one of those wonderful displays of Divine Power which we must admire, without being able, in the present state of our knowledge, to explain or understand. The Aurora has also been seen in high southern latitudes, but destitute of colour. In this situation it has been called, Aurora Australis, or Southern Daybreak.

PUBLISHED UNDER THE DIRECTION OF THE COMMITTEE OF GENERAL LITERATURE AND EDUCATION, APPOINTED BY THE SOCIETY FOR PROMOTING CHRISTIAN KNOWLEDGE.

PRICE ½d. PLAIN; 2d. COLOURED.

No. 2.]

G. BENTLEY AND CO., PRINTERS, BANGOR HOUSE, SHOE LANE.

Thirty Plates Illustrative of Natural Phenomena, etc.
London: The Society for Promoting Christian Knowledge, 1846. Gift of the Burndy Library.

This work contains beautiful color illustrations of various natural phenomena, including icebergs, waterspouts, and glaciers. Its publisher, the Society for Promoting Christian Knowledge, was founded in 1698 as an arm of the Church of England. The Society produced not only theological books but also works on popular science, travel, biography, and fiction.

detail

ADVENTURE WITH CURL-CRESTED TOUCANS.

PANORAMA FROM POINT SUBLIME

CLARENCE E. DUTTON (1841–1912)
Atlas to Accompany the Monograph on the Tertiary History of the Grand Canyon District. Washington, D.C.: U.S. Geological Survey, 1882.

Dutton's geological studies of the southwestern American plateaus provided brilliant interpretations of the physical structures of the Grand Canyon region. The oversize volume of maps and panoramas that accompanies his monograph on the region includes three double-page tinted lithographs, which together form this 180-degree view, as seen perhaps by the men sketching on the canyon's northern rim.

left

HENRY WALTER BATES (1825–1892)
The Naturalist on the River Amazons [*sic*]. 2 vols. London: John Murray, 1863. Gift of the Burndy Library.

The Englishman Henry W. Bates, fascinated by entomology since childhood, traveled with naturalist Alfred Russel Wallace to Brazil in 1848. He stayed for eleven years, collecting butterflies and other insects in the Amazon jungle. Despite ill health and unimaginable difficulties, he collected specimens of more than ten thousand animal species, eight thousand of which were new to Western science.

Edward S. Curtis (1868–1952)

The North American Indian. Seattle: E. S. Curtis; Cambridge, Mass.: The University Press, 1907–30. 20 vols. text, 20 portfolios of loose plates. Gift of Mrs. E. H. Harriman.

Edward S. Curtis, a professional photographer in Seattle, devoted his life to documenting what he perceived to be a vanishing race. His monumental publication presented to the public an extensive ethnographic study of numerous tribes, and his photographs remain memorable icons of the American Indian. The Smithsonian Libraries holds a complete set of his work, donated by Mrs. Edward H. Harriman, whose husband had conducted an expedition to Alaska, with Curtis as photographer, in 1899.

In the Air

Barthélemy Faujas de Saint-Fond
(1741–1819)
*Description des expériences de la machine aérostatique de
MM. de Montgolfier . . .* (Description of the experiments
of the Montgolfiers' aerial machine). 2 vols. Paris:
Chez Cuchet, 1783–84.

Travelers sailed into the sky for the first time in hot-air
balloons. The Montgolfier brothers, Joseph and Étienne,
early experimenters in balloon flight, organized the
first manned public ascension, piloted by Pilâtre de
Rozier and the Marquis d'Arlandes, in 1783. Faujas de
Saint-Fond's account and description of their exploits
was reprinted often, and the work is still consulted in
studying the advent of aeronautics. The Smithsonian
Libraries has both volumes of the first edition in fine
condition, a rare combination.

*Experience faite à Versaille, en presence de leurs Majestés et de la Famille Royale,
par M. Montgolfier, le 19. Sept. 1783.
La Machine Aérostatique avoit 57. Pieds de haut sur 41. de Diametre*

T.^a II.
Napoli 31 Marzo 1836
DILIGENZA PER LA LUNA

LEOPOLDO GALLUZZO AND GAETANO DURA
Altre Scoverte Fatte Nella Luna dal Sigr. Herschel or Great Astronomical Discoveries. Naples: L. Gatti e Dura, 1836.

This portfolio of hand-tinted lithographs purports to illustrate the "discovery of life on the moon." In 1836 Richard E. Locke, writing for the *New York Sun*, claimed that the noted British astronomer William Herschel had discovered life on the Moon. Flora and fauna included bat-men, moon maidens (with luna-moth wings), moon bison, and other extravagant life forms. Locke proposed an expedition to the Moon using a ship supported by hydrogen balloons.

Journeys over Land and Sea

THE INTERIOR OF THE PROJECTILE.

detail

JULES VERNE (1828–1905)
*From the Earth to the Moon Direct in Ninety-seven
Hours and Twenty Minutes, and a Trip around It.*
Trans. by Louis Mercier and Eleanor King.
New York: Scribner, Armstrong, 1874.

Long before men entered space, writers and artists
imagined their expeditions. Jules Verne's classic
science-fiction work on space flight first appeared in
English in 1874. His work remains of interest not only
to researchers studying the cultural history of space
flight but also to bibliophiles comparing the various
editions of Verne's books.

Leb Wohl! Da ist der Zeppelin, mit dem fahr nach Neuyork ich hin (Farewell! That is the zeppelin in which I'll travel to New York). [s.l.: s.n., 19??].

This charming early children's book celebrates a voyage on a zeppelin, from the Old World to the New.

You certainly have caught the lines of our ship. Donald A. Hall

CHARLES A. LINDBERGH (1902–1974)
We: The Famous Flier's Own Story of His Life and His Transatlantic Flight. New York: G. P. Putnam's Sons, 1927. William Burden Collection.

On May 21, 1927, Charles Lindbergh completed the first nonstop solo air crossing of the Atlantic, in 33 hours and 39 minutes. Lindbergh, who flew in a customized single-engine Ryan monoplane, the *Spirit of Saint Louis,* signed this copy, one from an edition of a thousand.

"WE"
By
CHARLES A. LINDBERGH

Authors Autograph Edition

One thousand copies of this edition have been printed for sale.
Each copy bears the autograph signature of the author.

This is No. 337
G. P. Putnam's Sons

Charles A. Lindbergh

FRED C. KELLY (1882–1959)
The Wright Brothers: A Biography Authorized by Orville Wright. New York: Harcourt, Brace, 1943.

Fred C. Kelly wrote the only authorized biography of the Wright brothers. George C. Page, an aeronautical engineer, sent his copy to prominent figures, especially from early aviation and space flight, for their autographs, with the intention of donating the book to the National Air and Space Museum of the Smithsonian. Among the 1,050 signatures are those of Charles Lindbergh and Dwight D. Eisenhower.

Journeys over Land and Sea

DICK CALKINS (1895–1962)
*Buck Rogers, 25th Century, featuring Buddy and Allura
in "Strange Adventures in the Spider Ship."* Chicago:
Pleasure Books, [ca. 1935]. Gift of Dr. Daniel J. Mason.

A number of pop-up books in the 1930s re-created
popular fairy tales and comic strips. Just as in early
printed books, monsters terrify travelers to new lands,
bizarre creatures terrorize voyagers in tales of outer
space. In this episode from the beloved science-fiction
comic strip *Buck Rogers,* Buck's friends Buddy and
Allura battle insectlike space aliens.

In the Air

GERALDINE CLYNE
The Jolly Jump-Ups Journey through Space.
Springfield, Mass.: McLoughlin Bros., 1952.
Gift of Daniel J. Mason.

Many of Clyne's colorful pop-up books center on the adventures of a typical American family of the 1950s, the Jolly Jump-Ups. In this book, one of a collection of nearly six hundred pop-up books and books with movable parts donated to the Cooper-Hewitt library in the 1980s, the Jolly Jump-Ups journey to Mars, where they encounter friendly aliens.

NEIL ARMSTRONG (B. 1930)
First on the Moon: A Voyage with Neil Armstrong,
Michael Collins, Edwin E. Aldrin, Jr. Boston: Little,
Brown, 1970. Michael Collins Collection.

On July 21, 1969, the Apollo XI Lunar Module *Eagle*
landed in the southwest corner of the Sea of Tranquil-
lity on the surface of the moon. The crew consisted of
Flight Comdr. Neil Armstrong, Col. Edwin Aldrin,
and Lt. Col. Michael Collins, who later became the
first director of the Smithsonian's National Air and
Space Museum. All members of the crew autographed
this copy.

Sheet Music

CHARLES POURNY
"Voyage au pays des étoiles" (Journey to the land of stars). Paris: Emile Benoit, [n.d.].

This song describes a young girl's dream of a journey into space by balloon.

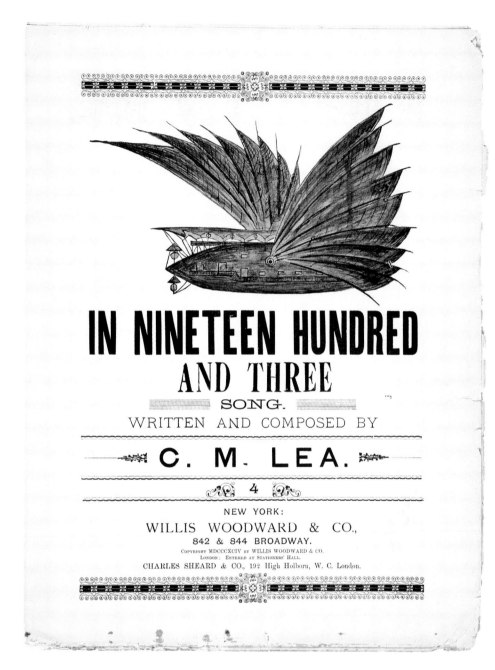

C. M. LEA
"In Nineteen Hundred and Three." New York:
Willis Woodward & Co., 1894.

The lyrics speculate about the possibility of powered,
controlled flight in 1903, surprisingly, the same year in
which the Wright brothers made their historic first flight.

In the Air

W. N. Freeman
"Three Hundred Years to Come." London: George and Manby, [n.d.].

Among the song's predictions of things to come is routine air travel in hot-air balloons. The traffic is terrible!

right

Clifford V. Baker
"A Trip to the Moon." Troy, N.Y.: Koninsky Music Co., 1907.

In this fanciful speculation about traveling to the moon in a dirigible, the travelers show no ill effects from their exposure to the cold vacuum of space. In fact, they appear to be greatly enjoying their expedition.

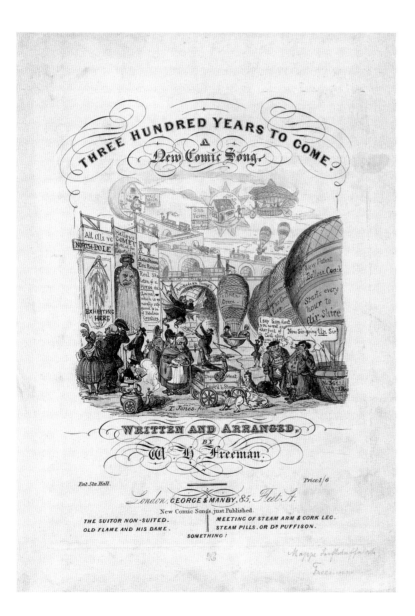

A TRIP to the MOON

by CLIFFORD V. BAKER.

ANOTHER GREAT DESCRIPTIVE MARCH SUCCESS BY THE COMPOSER OF THE FAMOUS "A TRIP TO NIAGARA FALLS"

KONINSKY MUSIC Co, 17 KING STREET, TROY, N.Y.

II. Journeys of the Mind

Scientific and intellectual discoveries—attempts to explain the unknown and often unseen—can be seen as journeys of the mind. Scientists tap their imaginations as they apply observation and experimentation to describe the natural world. At the Smithsonian, science and the history of science have been important from the beginning. Notable works of discovery in the physical and biological sciences and the history of technology form the strongest collections in the Smithsonian Libraries. Advances in fields from microscopy to space exploration, and from the earliest alchemy to the decoding of DNA, reflect the explorations of scientists beyond the observable universe.

The Smithsonian Institution began with the generosity of an English scientist, James Macie Smithson (1765–1829). Along with $508,318 in gold came Smithson's library and personal effects. While most items were lost in a devastating fire in 1865, a portion of Smithson's library remained intact and is in the Libraries collection today. (More information about Smithson and the founding of the Institution can be seen in the online exhibition "From Smithson to Smithsonian: The Birth of an Institution" (www.sil.si.edu/Exhibitions/Smithson-to-Smithsonian).

The natural-history library collections, the result of many scientific voyages and expeditions, contain rare illustrated works still used by scientists for taxonomic classification (identifying and naming species). Lavishly illustrated works in ornithology, botany, mineralogy, and zoology document pride in the discoveries being made with each venture. Works from the 1700s and early 1800s form the heart of the rare natural-history collections. A "golden age" for the subject, the period combined a flood of material from exotic lands, a newly developed system by Linnaeus for identifying and organizing it, and the peak of copperplate engraving and etching techniques. Many zoological and botanical treatises from the time have never been surpassed for beauty and accuracy. The great classifiers and describers announced to the world the variety and richness of species. As scientists looked closely to discover differences great or small, they preserved and studied specimens that have become part of the Smithsonian collections and which number more than 120 million items today. The work done in these collections in the nineteenth century established a sound foundation for the taxonomic description of flora and fauna. By the early twentieth century, the emperor of Japan, a skilled collector, could use the work of Mary Jane Rathbun, a nineteenth-century Smithsonian scientist, to identify crabs in the scientifically important Imperial Household collection. In turn,

Smithsonian scientists today, at the Environmental Research Center on Chesapeake Bay, refer to this 1901 catalog of the emperor's research collection.

In 1976 the Dibner Library of the History of Science and Technology, the largest special collection within the Smithsonian Libraries, was established with a gift to the nation from the Burndy Library, founded by Bern Dibner, an inventor, engineer, and book collector from Norwalk, Connecticut. The collection is particularly strong in the theoretical journeys of mathematics, physics, chemistry, and astronomy. The National Air and Space Museum Library began as a collection of publications that accompanied aeronautical artifacts. Augmenting research on both early space flight and regular flight, the library also assists the work of cultural and military historians. The Bella Landauer collection of aeronautical sheet music vividly conveys the great popularity and enthusiasm for manned flight and other scientific achievements among the general public.

Detail of "Moineau," from FRANÇOIS NICOLAS MARTINET, *Ornithologie* (Ornithology), 1773–92.

Classifiers and Describers

detail

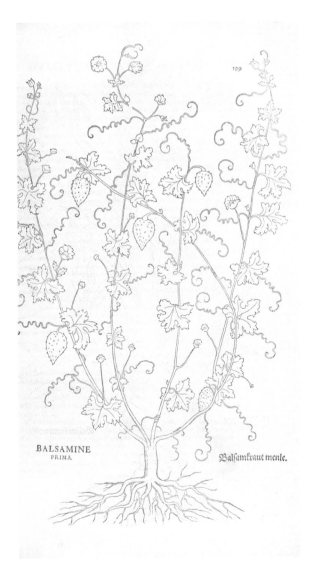

BALSAMINE
PRIMA.

Balsamkraut menle.

Leonhart Fuchs (1501–1566)
De historia stirpium (On the history of plants).
Basel: Isingrin, 1542. Gift of the Burndy Library.

In Renaissance times, medical treatments were based
on botany, but the herbals and other books available
to practitioners often inaccurately identified plants.
German physician Leonhart Fuchs deplored this
lack of knowledge and produced his book to rectify it.
Fuchs compiled the text from various classical sources
but added his own field observations, and the work is
famous for its more than five hundred woodcut illustrations, drawn by Heinrich Füllmaurer and Albrecht
Meyer and cut by Veit Rudolf Speckle. The Smithsonian Libraries copy is uncolored, which accentuates
the extraordinary beauty of line achieved by the artists
and demonstrates the Renaissance shift to the accurate
observation and drawing of plants from life. English
artist and designer William Morris owned a copy of
Fuchs's book and clearly took inspiration from it for
some of his own designs.

Le portraict de la Genette.

Genette.

Diuers metiers à Constantinoble.

Polissure du papier.

Il y a beaucoup de gents à Constantinoble qui font diuers mestiers que nous ignorons, car comme ils n'ont point l'impression, aussi est-ce vne reigle generalle que tous escripuent sur le papier bruni. Ils ne font point de papier en Turquie : mais l'achetent des marchands Italiens, qui le leur apportent par mer. Ceulx qui brunissent le papier, ont vn aix fort bien ioinct faict de pieces de buis, qui est quelque peu vouté en dedens, surquoy ils appuyent le papier, afin qu'en le frottant dessus il prenne lissure : mais pour le lisser ils encrent vne pierre de Cassidoine ou Iaspe au trauers d'vn baton long d'vne coudée, & tenants les deux bouts, frottent le papier auec la pierre dessus ledict aix de buis. Les Turcs ayment à auoir leurs espées qu'ils nomment Cimeterres, non pas ainsi luisantes comme les nostres, mais damasquinées : c'est à dire ternies de costé & d'autre : parquoy les armuriers sçauent detremper du sel Armoniac, & verd, & auec du vinaigre dedens quelque escuelle, ou ils mettent la pointe du Cimeterre : lequel estãt tenu debout, laissent couller de ladicte mixture

Fourbisseurs de Turquie.

tout

PIERRE BELON (1517–1564)

Les observations de plusieurs singularitez et choses memorables: Trouvées en Grèce, Asie, Judée, Egypte, Arabie, et autres pays estrange [sic] (Observations of many singular and memorable things found in Greece, Asia, Judea, Egypt, Arabia, and other foreign countries). Paris: Guillaume Cavellat, 1554. Bequest of Alexander Wetmore.

Trained as an apothecary and botanist, Belon is also recognized by modern science as the founder of comparative anatomy and embryology in animals. He was one of the first naturalist-explorers, and his observations made this book the most thoroughly documented account of the Levant to the time. First published in 1553, *Observations* was newly printed the following year with illustrations. The woodcuts include the first scientific description of the giraffe, known in medieval bestiaries as the "cameleopard."

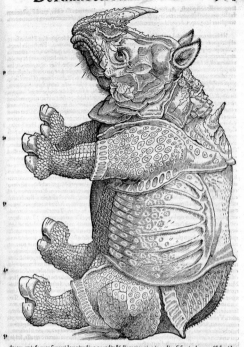

De Rhinocerote. A. Lib.I. 953

decem, ut ipse mensuraui, longitudine excedit: & diameter eius in radice sesquipalmum, (sesquido-
drantem intelligo,) superabar, Hæc ille, Inepte autem facit, primum quòd asinum Indicum ex Aristo-
tele scribens solipedem esse, mox rhinocerotem animal bisulcum interpretatur: deinde, quòd rhinocerotem & unicornem confundit: tertio, quòd archa uel archos Arabicum nomen faciens libro se-
cundo, (corruptum forte à uoce karas,) duodecimo principem interpretatur ac si Græca esset. Sed et
præteritas ista cornu, decem pedes excedens, rhinoceroti puto non conuenit, sed monoceroti carta-
zono, nam Oppianus rhinocerotis cornu paruum (hoc est breue, Gillius quoq paruum transfert)
esse scribit; ἐλαχυν δ᾽ ὑπερ ἰναψιν ἱππιν ἀτινδα λεσίξεα ἀκντιν, κνκχειλίκιοψ, ἀχριμυ ἔαρ. Quod si quis uerbum ἐλαχυν
non ad cornu quantitatem, sed ad loci distantiam referat, hoc sensu : paulò supra nares extremum nasum
crudele & acutissimum cornu oritur : nos tamen ex ipsa picturæ quam ad uiuum dedimus, propor-
tione, cornu breue esse conuincemus: nam cum supra nares incipiat, & multò infra aures desinat,

Ii 5

KONRAD GESNER (1516–1565)

Historia animalium (History of animals). 5 vols. in 3: vols. 1, 4, 5, Zurich: C. Froschouer, 1551–87; vols. 2, 3, Frankfurt: Ioannus Wechel, 1585–86. Gift of the Burndy Library.

In contrast to the bestiary tradition, the physician and polymath Konrad Gesner managed to reestablish the natural sciences on a recognizably scientific footing of observation, experimentation, and deduction. His encyclopedic work, compiled from folklore, ancient and medieval texts, and correspondence with a wide network of scholars, travelers, and natural philosophers, was tempered by his skepticism and an emphasis on direct observations. This copy, a mix of Zurich and Frankfurt imprints, is in a uniform blind-stamped pigskin binding dated 1599.

right

WILLEM PISO (1611–1678) AND GEORG MARGGRAF (1610–1644)

Historia naturalis Brasiliae (Natural history of Brazil). Leiden: F. Hackius; Amsterdam: L. Elzevir, 1648. Gift of Marcia Brady Tucker.

Willem Piso served as the physician of the Dutch settlement in Brazil from 1636 to 1644 and was a pioneer in tropical medicine and pharmacology. He studied the pharmacopoeia of the indigenous people and searched the jungle for medicinal plants. In advocating many native health practices, he was the first European to grasp the usefulness of numerous treatments using ipecacuanha, sassafras, sarsaparilla, guaiacum, and other plants. His findings constitute the first part of the *Historia naturalis Brasiliae;* the second and larger part is a broader natural history of the region by Georg Marggraf, Piso's assistant, and includes the first illustrations and descriptions of a variety of New World animals.

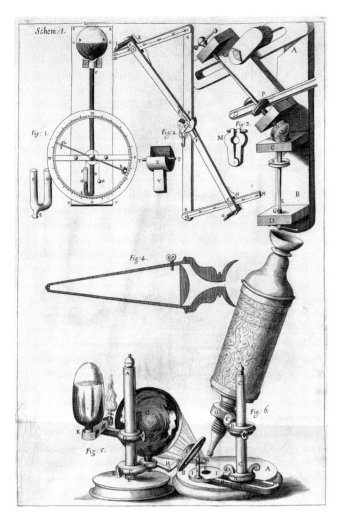

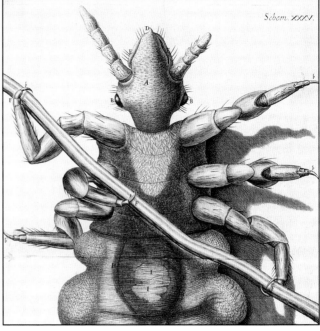

detail

Robert Hooke (1635–1703)

Micrographia: or Some Physiological Descriptions of Minute Bodies Made by Magnifying Glasses. London: printed by J. Martyn and J. Allestry, 1665. Gift of the Burndy Library.

Curator of experiments at the Royal Society of London, Hooke published his *Micrographia* (literally, "Little Drawings") to record a series of observations he had made with a microscope. Like Galileo's *Sidereus nuncius* (see p. 126), the *Micrographia* presented such a panoply of new observations with dramatic visual effect that it had an enormous influence on the development of science. Hooke was the first scientist to use the word "cell" and to speculate on its function. The detailed plates in *Micrographia* were so popular that they were reprinted continually in other books up to the nineteenth century.

Journeys of the Mind

Maria Sibylla Merian (1647–1717)

Metamorphosis insectorum surinamensium (Transformations of the insects of Surinam). Amsterdam: for the author by G. Valck, [1705].

Maria Sibylla Merian, the daughter, sister, and wife of artists and engravers, lived a most unconventional life: she became an artist herself, left her husband to join a Protestant sect, and voyaged at the age of fifty to the Dutch colony of Surinam. Merian, who worked professionally under her own name, spent two years in the jungle observing, collecting, and drawing insects and plants. Despite a few errors, her *Metamorphosis*, published after her return, is a masterpiece of both art and science. Using a vivid, pleasingly ornate artistic style, she was the first to record the full life cycle of many species of butterflies and moths.

François Nicolas Martinet (1731–1790?)
[*Ornithologie*] (Ornithology). [Paris: s.n., 1773–92].
Gift of Marcia Brady Tucker.

Martinet, though trained as an engineer, was another
of the great eighteenth-century engravers, producing
hundreds of plates for Brisson's *Ornithologie* and
Buffon's *Histoire naturelle,* among other works. Carrying on the success of his ornithological illustrations,
he and his son engraved and issued independently at
least two series of bird plates from the 1770s into the
1790s. The 174 numbered plates in this volume are
especially charming for their delicate coloring and
occasional Parisian backgrounds.

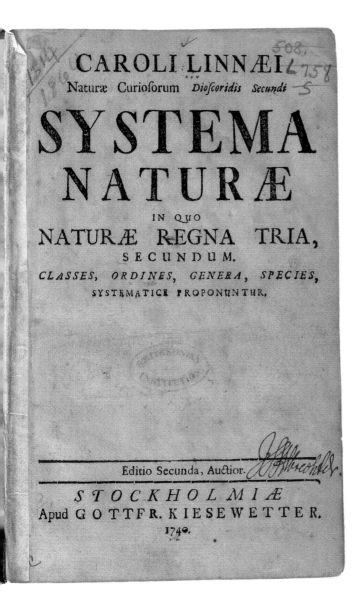

Carolus Linnaeus (Carl von Linné, 1707–1778)
Systema naturae (System of nature). 2nd ed. Stockholm: Kiesewetter, 1740.

World explorers brought back to Europe so many exotic plant and animal specimens that chaos loomed for the eighteenth-century naturalists attempting to identify, classify, and communicate what they had gathered. Linnaeus made a great contribution to science by developing systems of classification and nomenclature to organize these processes. His principles of organization, including most especially his system of binomial nomenclature, provided essential tools for making sense of the natural world. The practice of taxonomy (naming and classifying species) and systematics (the classification of species into higher groups) continues at the National Museum of Natural History today and still relies on Linnaeus's classic work. The tenth edition (1758–59), which the Libraries holds in multiple copies, was chosen as the starting point for zoological nomenclature. This much rarer copy of the second edition is from the library of Lorenz Oken (1799–1851), a renowned German natural scientist.

Marcus Elieser Bloch (1723–1799)

[*Allgemeine Naturgeschichte der Fische*] (General natural history of fishes). 4 vols. and 4 atlases. Berlin: Hr. Hesse, 1782–95.

Bloch's work is one of the high points in the history of ichthyology, both graphically and taxonomically. It is still in use as a standard reference for identification. Bloch described fishes from all over the world, relying on numerous contacts around the globe. In all, he listed more than 169 new species. A French edition, published in Berlin in 1785–97, allowed the work to reach a wider audience. Various engravers produced the plates in a remarkably consistent style over a twelve-year period. The Smithsonian is one of only nine institutions in the world to hold a complete set of the original German editions and one of only two libraries to hold both the German and the French.

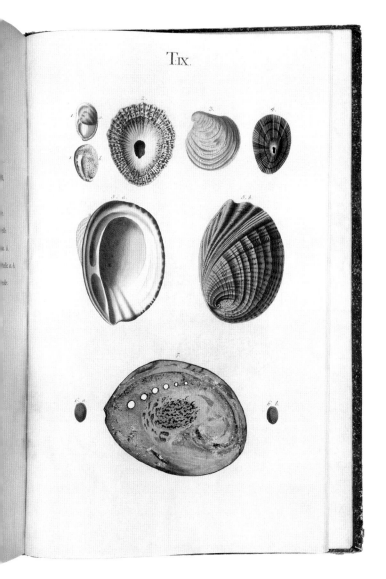

Joachim Johann Nepomuk A. Spalowsky
(1752–1797)

Prodromus in systema historiam testaceorum (Introduction to a systematic classification of shelled animals). Vienna: Ignaz Alberti's Wittwe, 1795. [1801 issue].

Elegantly combining art and science, Spalowsky's *Prodromus* presents descriptions of new mollusk species accompanied by strikingly beautiful illustrations, some of them painstakingly layered with gold and silver leaf under watercolor to reproduce the effect of iridescence. This book, in the 1801 issue with a contemporary binding, is one of the rarest published works on mollusks.

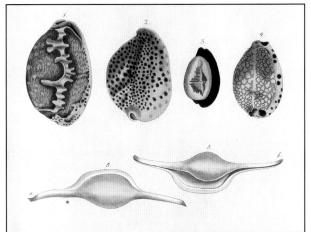

detail

Compound salt, of carbonate of zinc and hydrate of zinc 990.3
Water, in the state of moisture - - 2.5
Carbonate of zinc and carbonate of lead - 7.2
          1000.0

It may be thought some corroboration of the system here offered, that, if we admit the proportions which it indicates, the remote elements of this ore, while they are regular parts of their immediate products, by whose subsequent union this ore is engendered, are also regular fractions of the ore itself: thus,

The carbonic acid - - - $= \frac{1}{10}$
The water - - - $= \frac{2}{10}$
The calx of zinc - - - $= \frac{4}{10}$

Hereby displaying that sort of regularity, in every point of view of the object, which so wonderfully characterises the works of nature, when beheld in their true light.

If this calamine does consist of carbonate of zinc and hydrate of zinc, in the regular proportions above supposed, little doubt can exist of its being a true chemical combination of these two matters, and not merely a mechanical mixture of them in a pulverulent state; and, if so, we may indulge the hope of some day meeting with this ore in regular crystals.

If the theory here advanced has any foundation in truth, the discovery will introduce a degree of rigorous accuracy and certainty into chemistry, of which this science was thought to be ever incapable, by enabling the chemist, like the geometrician, to rectify by calculation the unavoidable errors of his manual operations, and by authorising him to discriminate from the essential elements of a compound, those products of its analysis whose quantity cannot be reduced to any admissible proportion.

A certain knowledge of the exact proportions of the constituent

principles of bodies, may likewise open to our view harmonious analogies between the constitutions of related objects, general laws, &c. which at present totally escape us. In short, if it is founded in truth, its enabling the application of mathematics to chemistry, cannot but be productive of material results.*

3. By the application of the foregoing theory to the experiments on the electrical calamine, its elements will appear to be,

Quartz - - - $\frac{1}{4}$
Calx of zinc - - - $\frac{3}{4}$

A small quantity of the calamine having escaped the action of the vitriolic acid, and remained undecomposed, will account for the slight excess in the weight of the quartz.

4. The exhalation of these calamines at the blowpipe, and the flowers which they diffuse round them on the coal, are probably not to be attributed to a direct volatilization of them. It is more probable that they are the consequences of the dis-oxidation of the zinc calx, by the coal and the inflammable matter of the flame, its sublimation in a metallic state, and instantaneous recalcination. And this alternate reduction and combustion, may explain the peculiar phosphoric appearance exhibited by calces of zinc at the blowpipe.

The apparent sublimation of the common flowers of zinc at the instant of their production, though totally unsublimable afterwards, is certainly likewise but a deceptive appearance. The reguline zinc, vaporized by the heat, rises from the crucible as a metallic gas, and is, while in this state, converted to a calx. The flame which attends the process is a proof of it; for flame is a mass of vapour, ignited by the production of fire within itself.

* It may be proper to say, that the experiments have been stated *precisely* as they turned out, and have not been in the *least degree* bent to the system.

James Smithson (1765–1829)

"A chemical analysis of some calamines." In *Philosophical Transactions of the Royal Society of London, For the year MDCCCIII, Part I.* [Vol. 93]. London: printed by W. Bulmer, 1803. From the Smithson Library collection.

James Lewis Macie Smithson was a gentleman-scientist, educated at Oxford and interested in chemistry, mineralogy, and geology. His twenty-seven scientific papers, published in the Royal Society's *Philosophical Transactions* and *Thomson's Annals of Philosophy,* include this one on the mineral (a form of zinc carbonate) that was later named "smithsonite" in his honor. Smithson bequeathed $508,318 in gold as well as his library and personal effects to the United States, but many items were lost in a devastating fire in 1865. Approximately 115 titles survived, including several copies of this corrected offprint, and they are now in the Smithsonian Libraries Special Collections. For more information about Smithson and the founding of the Institution, see the online exhibition "From Smithson to Smithsonian: The Birth of an Institution" (www.sil.si.edu/Exhibitions/Smithson-to-Smithsonian).

Gryllus ſtridulus Fabr.

GEORG WOLFGANG FRANZ PANZER
(1755–1829)
Faunae insectorum germanicae initia (Elements of
the insect fauna of Germany). 18 vols. Nuremberg:
Felseckerschen Buchhandlung, 1796–1813.

Entomology is a fertile field for artists as well as
scientists and was recognized as such in the 1700s.
Illustrated by Jacob Sturm (1771–1848), one of the
period's best entomological artist/engravers, with
more than 2,600 hand-colored plates of individual,
life-size insects, Panzer's work was issued in 109 parts
over a period of seventeen years. Issued as a serial
publication, a common pattern for illustrated natural-
history works in the eighteenth and nineteenth
centuries, complete sets are scarce. The Smithsonian
Libraries has one of them, in contemporary bindings.

details

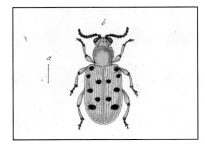 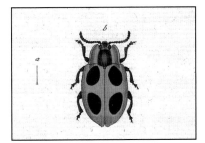 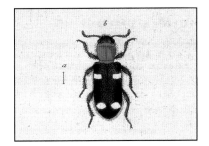

Vitis vulpina.

Nikolaus Joseph Jacquin (1727–1817)
Plantarum rariorum horti caesarei Schoenbrunnensis descriptiones et icones (Descriptions and pictures of rare plants in the gardens of Schönbrunn castle). 4 vols. [Vienna]: C. F. Wappler; London: B. & J. White; Leiden: S. & J. Luchtmans, 1797–1804.

The late 1700s saw a great enthusiasm throughout Europe for importing and cultivating rare and exotic plants from newly explored regions of the world. Jacquin, a Dutchman of French extraction, produced many of the great florilegia, or flower books, of the period as director of the Austrian imperial gardens and natural history collections. Collectively his works presented a multitude of new species descriptions and some 2,700 plates of plants, many of them never before depicted. This magnificent four-volume folio, published in fewer than two hundred copies, contains five hundred detailed engravings of plants from South Africa, the Americas, and other distant regions, all of which were grown in the royal gardens of Schönbrunn.

right

Henry David Thoreau (1817–1862)
Walden; or, Life in the Woods. Boston: Ticknor and Fields, 1854. Donated by Spencer F. Baird.

Embraced as a precursor of the modern environmentalist movement, Thoreau's work emphasizes an appreciation of nature for itself rather than as a resource to be exploited—a sharp departure from the prevailing economic and religious views of the period. Thoreau inscribed and gave this copy to Spencer F. Baird, a young natural scientist who had been selected just a few years earlier as Assistant Secretary of the newly founded Smithsonian Institution. Baird had been introduced to Thoreau by Ralph Waldo Emerson in 1847.

WALDEN;

OR,

LIFE IN THE WOODS.

By HENRY D. THOREAU,

AUTHOR OF "A WEEK ON THE CONCORD AND MERRIMACK RIVERS."

I do not propose to write an ode to dejection, but to brag as lustily as chanticleer in the morning, standing on his roost, if only to wake my neighbors up. — Page 92.

BOSTON:

TICKNOR AND FIELDS.

M DCCC LIV.

ON

THE ORIGIN OF SPECIES

BY MEANS OF NATURAL SELECTION,

OR THE

PRESERVATION OF FAVOURED RACES IN THE STRUGGLE
FOR LIFE.

By CHARLES DARWIN, M.A.,

FELLOW OF THE ROYAL, GEOLOGICAL, LINNÆAN, ETC., SOCIETIES;
AUTHOR OF 'JOURNAL OF RESEARCHES DURING H. M. S. BEAGLE'S VOYAGE
ROUND THE WORLD.'

LONDON:
JOHN MURRAY, ALBEMARLE STREET.
1859.

The right of Translation is reserved.

CHARLES DARWIN (1809–1882)
On the Origin of Species by Means of Natural Selection.
London: John Murray, 1859. Gift of the Burndy
Library.

Destined by his family for the clergy, Charles Darwin
served, unpaid, as a naturalist on the H.M.S. *Beagle*
during a British naval surveying voyage to South
America in 1831. Only later, after his return, did the
significance of his observations lead Darwin inexorably
to his revolutionary conclusions. He was not the only
scientist to advance the theory of evolution, but he
spent twenty years working out its operation through
the processes of natural selection before publishing
Origin in 1859. The book caused a sensation, and although the fact of evolution is irrefutable, the contro-
versy over the mechanism continues unabated.

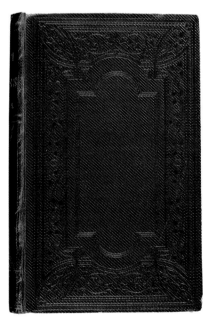

CHARLES DARWIN (1809–1882)
Autograph letter [to W. Whitaker], signed and dated
March 16, 1880. Gift of the Burndy Library.

As an old man, only two years before his death, Darwin
wrote: "Dear Sir / I must send one line to thank you
for thinking to send me the article on inheritance,
which is a subject which always interests me. Dear Sir /
Yours faithfully & [?] / Ch. Darwin."

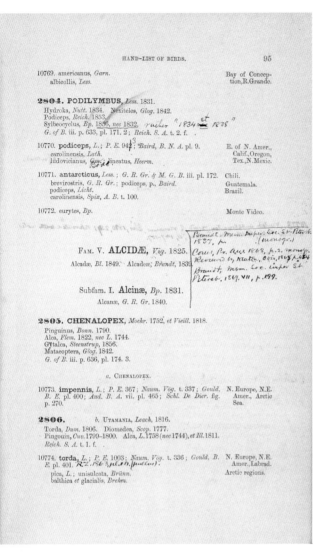

GEORGE ROBERT GRAY (1808–1872)
Hand-list of the Genera and Species of Birds . . . in the British Museum (Natural History). 3 vols. London: by order of the Trustees, 1869–71.

Although an important reference work in ornithological taxonomy, Gray's *Hand-list* is not in itself rare. This copy, however, was owned and annotated by Elliott Coues (1842–1899), the premier American ornithologist of the period, after the Smithsonian's Spencer F. Baird (1833–1889). Coues studied informally under Baird and worked with the expedition collections at the Smithsonian throughout his life. Books interleaved to provide space for annotations, linking the text to specimens in museum collections and to related taxonomic works, are not uncommon in the Smithsonian Libraries holdings. In an inscription Coues exhorted later owners of this copy (who included book collector Evan Morton Evans and ornithologists John Eliot Thayer and Robert Cushman Murphy) to continue the annotations.

PARADISEA RAGGIANA, *Sclater.*

JOHN GOULD (1804–1881)
The Birds of New Guinea and the Adjacent Papuan Islands. 5 vols. London: H. Sotheran, 1875–88. Gift of John H. Phipps.

Like all of Gould's works, *The Birds of New Guinea,* completed by Richard Bowdler Sharpe after Gould's death in 1881, is both beautiful and scientifically important. In it are described and illustrated many exotic species of birds, including the birds of paradise unique to New Guinea—bowerbirds, parrots, and others previously unknown to Western science. Its 310 hand-colored lithographs were largely the work of William Hart, who produced the final watercolors based on Gould's sketches and transferred them to the printing stone. This and other volumes in the John H. Phipps donation (1980) enriched and complemented the already fine collections that support ornithological research within the Institution.

A CALIFORNIA HOSPITAL FOR INJURED BIRDS
erected and maintained by Mrs. Harriet W. Myers of Los Angeles

Thomas Gilbert Pearson (1873–1943)

The Bird Study Book. Garden City, N.Y.: Doubleday, Page, 1917.

Pearson, a famous southern naturalist, was one of the founders and later president of the National Association of Audubon Societies (now the National Audubon Society). He also founded the International Council for Bird Preservation and established many school libraries throughout his native North Carolina by donating natural history books to school superintendents. His early work on bird conservation is important to the mission of the Smithsonian Migratory Bird Center at the National Zoological Park as well as to the history of the conservation movement in the United States. The Smithsonian Libraries' copy is signed by the author.

right

Seibutsugaku Gokenkyūjo

Crabs of Sagami Bay, collected by His Majesty the Emperor of Japan. Honolulu: East West Center Press, 1965.

This volume is one of several published by Emperor Hirohito (1901–1989), an avid and lifelong marine biologist. Hirohito himself collected the crabs illustrated in this instructive volume and identified them in his palace laboratory. With its complex seabed and warm and cold currents, Sagami Bay is a site well known for its diverse marine life.

Journeys of the Mind

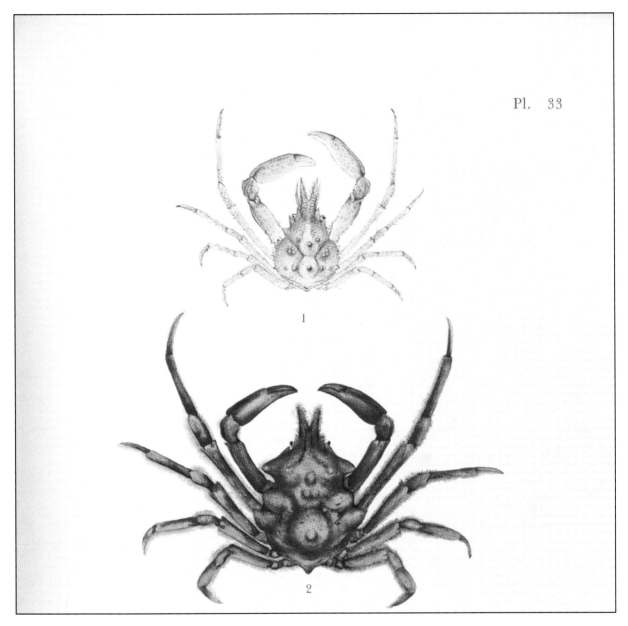

Pl. 33

1

2

detail

JOHN W. TAYLOR (B. 1931)
Birds of the Chesapeake Bay: Paintings by John W. Taylor
with Natural Histories and Journal Notes by the Artist.
Baltimore: Johns Hopkins University Press, 1992.

This book is unique in the Smithsonian Libraries collections in its artistic portrayals of many birds of the Chesapeake Bay. The author, a naturalist who lives along the shores of the bay, recorded much about the habits of these and other birds for more than thirty years. Taylor's ornithologically accurate, full-color drawings depict rarely seen birds that inhabit the area. With each drawing, Taylor gives a natural history of the bird and describes efforts to maintain the bird's habitat from encroaching development.

Explaining the Heavens

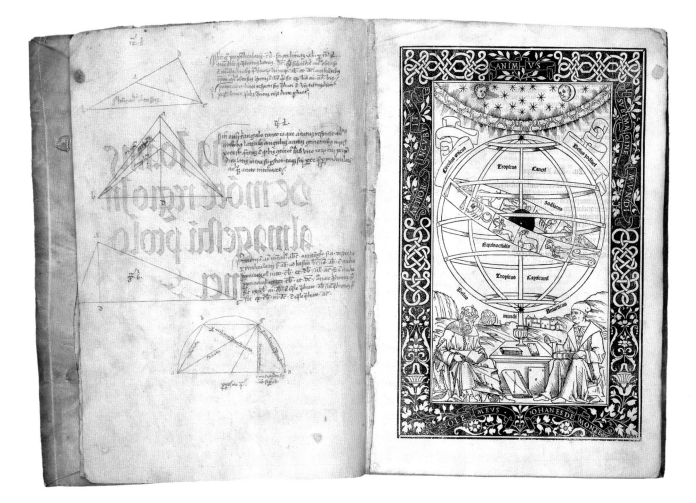

REGIOMONTANUS (JOHANN MÜLLER, 1436–1476)
Epitoma in almagestum Ptolomei (Abridgment of Ptolemy's *Almagest).* Venice: Johannes Hamman, 1496. Gift of the Burndy Library.

Austrian astronomer Georg Peurbach began a new Latin translation in 1460 of Ptolemy's compendium of Greek astronomical knowledge, and Regiomontanus, a German astronomer and mathematician, completed it before 1463. The authors clarified obscure passages and offered a concise and comprehensible summary of the *Almagest.* The work, marking the first appearance in print of Ptolemy's treatise, had an unprecedented impact on Renaissance astronomers and played a key role in the development of modern astronomy. The Smithsonian copy is heavily annotated and contains numerous mathematical drawings.

Regiomontanus (Johann Müller, 1436–1476)

Kalendarium (Calendar book). Augsburg: Erhard Ratdolt, 1499. Gift of the Burndy Library.

Regiomontanus, one of the first publishers of astronomical material, developed an almanac series that was popular enough to continue after his death. The almanacs contained planetary positions for a particular year as calculated from astronomical tables, freeing astronomers from performing the laborious task themselves. This 1499 copy contains numerous annotations to the almanac and its eclipse predictions.

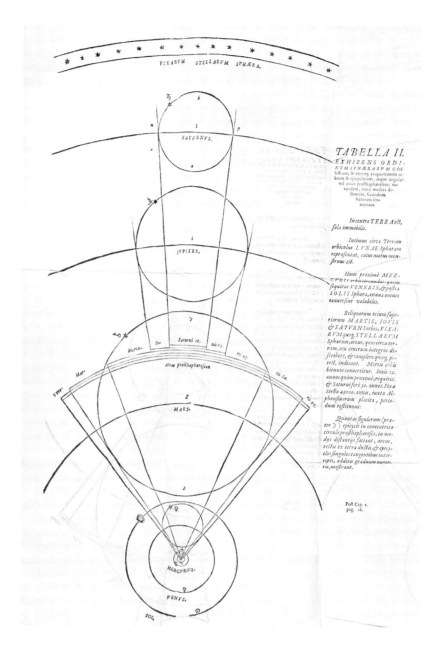

FIXARVM STELLARVM SPHÆRA.

SATVRNVS.

IVPITER.

Saturni 12.

Arcus prostbaphærefeon

MARS.

MERCVRIVS.

VENVS.

SOL.

TABELLA II.
EXHIBENS ORDI-
NEM SPHÆRARVM COE-
lestium, & veteris proportionem or-
bium & epicyclorum, atque angulos
vel arcus prosthaphæreseon eo-
rundem, iuxta medias di-
stantias, secundum
Veterum sen-
tentiam.

In centro TERRA est,
sola immobilis.

Intimus circa Terram
orbiculus LVNÆ Sphæram
repræsentat, cuius motus men-
struus est.

Hunc proximè MER-
CVRII orbem circumdat, quem
sequitur VENERIS, & postea
SOLIS Sphæra, annua omnes
conuersione volubiles.

Reliquorum trium supe-
riorum MARTIS, IOVIS
& SATVRNI orbes, FIXA-
RVM quoq; STELLARVM
Sphæram, arcus, quos circa terram, ceu centrum integros de-
feribere, & complere quæq; pu-
teit, indicant. Martis orbis
biennio conuertitur. Iovis 12.
annos quàm proximè, requirit.
& Saturni ferè 30. annos. Fixa
Stella 49000. annis, iuxta Al-
phonsinorum placita, perio-
dum restituunt:

Quantas singulorum (præ-
ter ☽) epicycli in concentrico
circulo prosthaphæreses, in me-
dijs distantijs faciant, arcus,
rectis ex terra ductis, & epicy-
clos singulos tangentibus inter-
cepti, additis graduum nume-
ris, monstrant.

Post Cap. 1.
pag. 11.

JOHANNES KEPLER (1571–1630)

Prodromus dissertationum cosmographicarum (Prologue to a dissertation on a description of the universe). Tübingen: Georg Gruppenbach, 1596. Gift of the Burndy Library.

Imposing mathematical harmony on the skies, Kepler proposed that the planetary orbits nested one inside the other, with each planet (at the time, thought to be six) alternating with one of the five Platonic "solids"— geometric figures such as the cube. This elegant model addressed both the number of planets and the spacing of their orbits. Kepler's idea, while not fully worked out, clarified the spatial organization of the solar system while arguing that geometry was an innate part of the divine plan of creation.

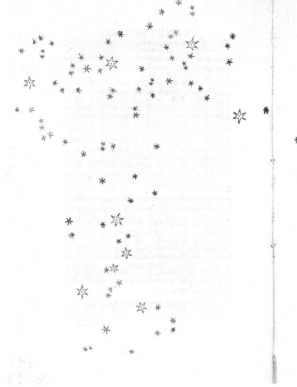

Quòd tertio loco à nobis fuit obseruatum, est ipsius-
met LACTEI Circuli essentia, seu materies, quam Per-
spicilli beneficio adeò ad sensum licet intueri, vt & alter-
cationes omnes, quæ per tot sæcula Philosophos excrucia-
runt ab oculata certitudine dirimantur, nosque à verbosis
disputationibus liberemur. Est enim GALAXYA nihil
aliud, quam innumerarum Stellarum coaceruatim consi-
tarum congeries; in quamcunq; enim regionem illius Per-
spicilium dirigas, statim Stellarum ingens frequentia se se
in conspectum profert, quarum complures satis magnæ, ac
valde conspicuæ videntur; sed exiguarum multitudo pror-
sus inexplorabilis est.

At cum non tantum in GALAXYA lacteus ille candor,
veluti albicantis nubis spectetur, sed complures consimilis
coloris areolæ sparsim per æthera subfulgeant, si in illarum
quamlibet Specillum conuertas Stellarum constipatarum
cætum

GALILEO GALILEI (1564–1642)
Sidereus nuncius magna (The great starry messenger).
Venice: T. Baglionum, 1610. Gift of the Burndy
Library, ex-collection Herbert McLean Evans.

Shortly after the invention of the telescope, Galileo in
1609 constructed one for himself and turned it to the
heavens. He quickly published this brief account of his
amazing discoveries, the first work of modern observational astronomy. In it, Galileo describes his revolutionary sightings of craters on the Moon, individual
stars in the Milky Way, and the Galilean satellites, the
four largest moons of Jupiter. Publication of *Sidereus
nuncius* began a chain of events that shook the foundation of European thought and launched an intellectual
voyage that would take us deeper into the universe.

right

GALILEO GALILEI (1564–1642)
Systema cosmicum (System of the world). Leiden:
I. A. Huguetan, 1641. Gift of the Burndy Library.

Systema cosmicum is the Latin translation of Galileo's
great 1632 treatise, *Dialogo sopra i due massimi sistemi del
mondo . . .* (Dialogue concerning the two chief world
systems). Galileo set the *Dialogo* as a conversation
among three people about the problems and merits of
the classical Earth-centered model of the solar system
versus the newer Sun-centered one. Galileo's endorsement of the latter arrangement so infuriated papal
authorities that he was kept under house arrest for
the remainder of his life. He first published his treatise
in Italian, as an appeal to the larger public, and then
again in 1641, in Latin, the language of the intellectual
world. This copy was owned by the Dutch Protestant
theologian Alhart de Raedt (b. 1645), who annotated
the book extensively.

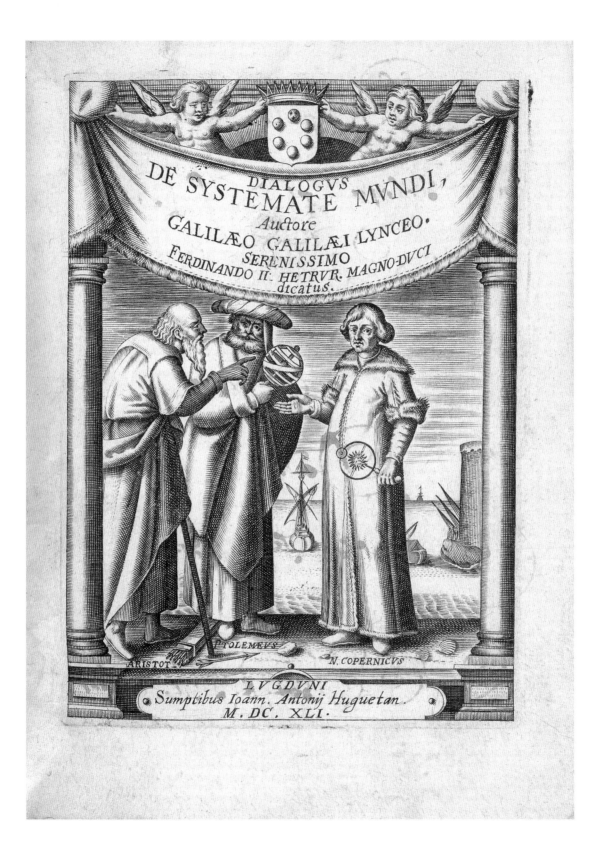

DIALOGVS
DE SYSTEMATE MVNDI,
Auctore
GALILÆO GALILÆI LYNCEO.
SERENISSIMO
FERDINANDO II: HETRVR. MAGNO-DVCI
dicatus.

ARISTOT   PTOLEMEVS   N. COPERNICVS

LVGDVNI
Sumptibus Ioann. Antonij Huguetan.
M. DC. XLI.

JOHANN ESAIAS SILBERSCHLAG (1721–1791)
Theorie der am 23 Julii, 1762, erschienen Feuer-Kugel
(Theory on the July 23, 1762, appearance of a fireball).
Magdeburg, Stendal, and Leipzig: Commercien-Rath
Hechtel, 1764. Paneth Collection.

In 1762 a large fireball entered the Earth's atmosphere
and exploded over Germany. Silberschlag provided a
good description of the event along with engravings
of meteors, the fireball's path, and its ultimate fiery
explosion. Not until the 1800s did scientists begin to
concede that fireballs and meteorites might have extra-
terrestrial origins. Prior to that, it was difficult to con-
ceive how boulders could fall from the sky, and many
believed that meteorites were simply rocks struck by
lightning.

right

JOHANNES HEVELIUS (1611–1687)
Machinæ coelestis (Celestial machines, or astronomical
instruments). 2 vols. Danzig: S. Reininger, 1673–79.
Gift of the Burndy Library, ex-collection Herbert
McLean Evans.

Hevelius's personal observatory in Danzig was the best-
equipped facility of its kind in the world. A champion
of the "long-focus" telescope, which could reach more
than 100 feet in length, Hevelius was an expert builder
who constructed many of his own instruments. The
first volume of this work describes his "celestial machines" in great detail, and its engravings often depict
Hevelius using the devices, frequently in concert with
his wife and collaborator, Elisabetha.

A. Steck Delin.   J. Saal Sculps.

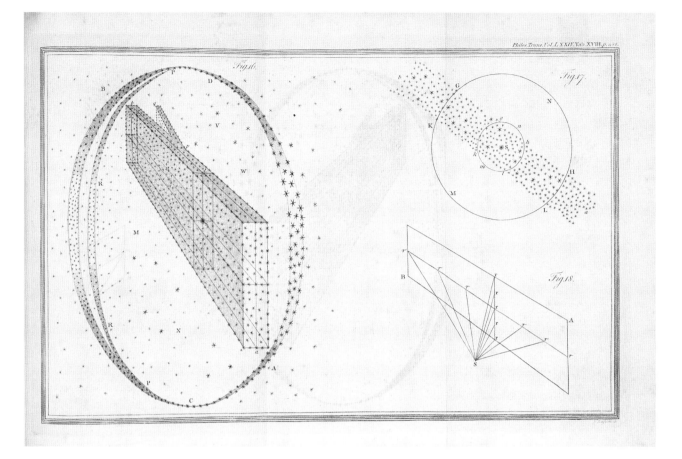

WILLIAM HERSCHEL (1738–1822)
"Account of Some Observations Tending to Investigate the Construction of the Heavens." In *Philosophical Transactions of the Royal Society of London.* Vol. 74 (1784). From the U.S. Patent Office Library.

A great pioneer in the study of the stars, William Herschel was appointed private astronomer to the king of England in recognition of his discovery of the planet Uranus (1781). In this paper, he made his first, not entirely successful attempt at a scientific explanation of the structure of the Milky Way galaxy, opening a debate that continues to this day. The folding plate illustrates his concept of how the galaxy would appear to an outside observer. Herschel also claimed that dim nebulous patches in the sky were galaxies just like our own.

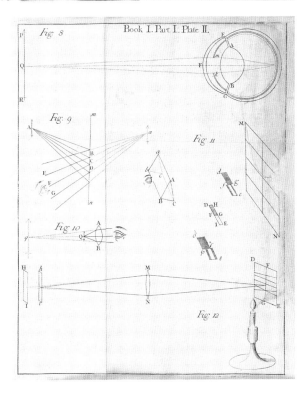

Isaac Newton (1642–1727)

Opticks, or, A Treatise of the Reflections, Refractions, Inflections and Colours of Light. 2nd ed. London: W. and J. Innys, 1718. Gift of the Burndy Library.

When Newton presented his concepts about the behavior and characteristics of light, particularly that white light is composed of a spectrum of colors, he posed a number of questions intended to stimulate further research in a section known as "The Queries." In the 1718 revision of his 1704 work, Newton extended his original sixteen queries to thirty-one; these discourses were considered the most provocative parts of the book. Through the queries, Newton speculated that a fluid, or "aether," pervaded all of space and provided the medium through which light could travel. Robert Smith (1689–1768), Plumian Professor of Astronomy at Cambridge University and author of the most influential textbook on optics in the eighteenth century, owned this copy and annotated it heavily.

ALTA VISTA STATION — JUPITER

As seen in the Pattinson Equatorial with magnifying power 350 at 23ʰ Sid. Time on September 4ᵗʰ 1856

C.P.S. delt.   J. Basire, lith.

ALTA VISTA STATION — JUPITER

At 23ʰ 30ᵐ Sid. Time on September 5ᵗʰ 1856. Meridian 170° difference from drawing of Sepᵗ 4ᵗʰ

CHARLES PIAZZI SMYTH (1819–1900)
Report on the Teneriffe Astronomical Experiment of 1856.
London: printed by Richard Taylor and William
Francis, 1858.

Piazzi Smyth was the first astronomer to advocate
seriously that astronomical observations would be
greatly improved if done at high altitudes. His report
to the British Admiralty of his expedition to the Canary
Islands had a great influence on the next generation of
astronomers, including Samuel P. Langley (1834–1906),
third Secretary of the Smithsonian. Piazzi Smyth sent
this copy to Langley, and it includes annotations by
the two men as well as a glued-in spectrum by Piazzi
Smyth and a letter from him to Langley.

LES ÉTOILES FILANTES OBSERVÉES EN BALLON

James Glaisher (1809–1903), with
Camille Flammarion, W. de Fonvielle,
and Gaston Tissandier
Voyages aériens (Travels in the air). Paris: L. Hachette,
1870. Collection of Gaston Tissandier.

A founder of the Aeronautical Society of Great Britain,
Glaisher described the first recorded balloon ascensions
undertaken specifically for scientific research. Glaisher
and his colleagues studied atmospherics and meteorol-
ogy, and they nearly died from asphyxiation and hypo-
thermia when their balloon rose too high.

detail

AURORA. GUILDFORD. OCT. 24. 1870.
FROM A WATER COLOUR DRAWING.

Mintern Bros lith.

JOHN RAND CAPRON (1829–1888)
Auroræ: Their Characters and Spectra. London
and New York: E. & F. N. Spon, 1879. Gift of
the Burndy Library.

Early voyagers to the polar regions often saw the
northern lights, a remarkable luminous display that
some considered to be mists emanating from the ground.
Capron was one of the first scientists to discuss the
chemical and physical nature of the phenomenon. By
the 1950s, it was accepted that the northern lights are
caused by the interaction of high-energy electrons from
the Sun with atoms in the Earth's upper atmosphere.

Willy Ley (1906–1969)
Die Möglichkeit der Weltraumfahrt (The feasibility of interplanetary travel). Leipzig: Hachmeister und Thal, 1928.

Ley, a paleontologist, engineer, and theorist on conditions on other planets and in space, edited this book of essays written by famous rocket scientists, including Hermann Oberth, Walter Hohmann, and Guido von Pirquet.

— 307 —

primieren und durch die Hochdruckgasleitung neuerdings der Düse zuzuführen. So entsteht ein Kreisprozeß, der durch die unter Ent-

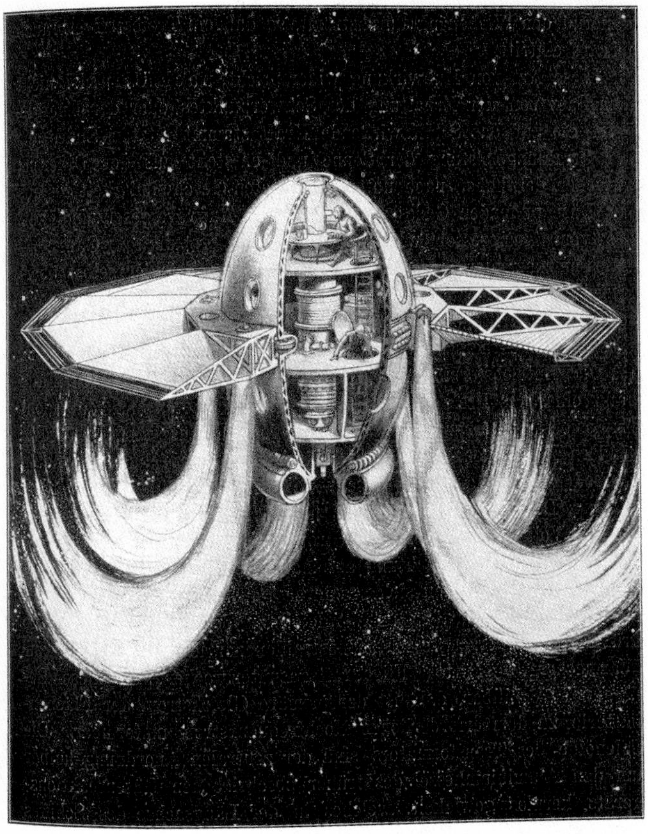

Abb. 68.
Die Elektronenrakete Franz Abdon Ulinskis [1]).

[1]) Entnommen aus der Zeitschrift „Die Rakete", dem Organ des Vereins für Raumschiffahrt E. V. Breslau vom 15. 9. 27.

20*

DR. ROBERT H. GODDARD

ROBERT HUTCHINGS GODDARD (1882–1945)
*Rockets, Comprising "A Method of Reaching Extreme
Altitudes" and "Liquid-Propellant Rocket Development."*
New York: American Rocket Society, [1946].

This volume is a republication of Robert Goddard's
pioneering research in liquid-fuel rocket development.
Goddard, considered the founding father of modern
rocketry, laid the groundwork for America's space
program. The Smithsonian supported his research
beginning in 1916 and published his first book on
rocketry in 1919. The Institution, despite mockery
from skeptics, published further research in 1936.

III. Journeys of the Imagination

Authors and artists explore the terrain of the imagination when producing books. Whether the result is a graphic or literary work of art, a scientific treatise, or a description of uncharted continents, each author enters what is, to him or her, previously undiscovered land. For some, the book is an end in itself, a revelation of the mind's voyages; for others, it is a tool for announcing products or services to the public. The Smithsonian Libraries collect examples of design and visual arts in both fine art books and mass-produced titles. The collections feature achievements in printing, graphics, and binding, chosen for the intrinsic value of their contents and their beauty as works of art. Classic works at the Smithsonian come from the fields of architecture, the decorative arts, and design, and include world's fair and exposition literature and early trade catalogs. In each effort, to attract and engage the reader's attention, artists or designers translated their ideas into two-dimensional formats. They cleverly invented special effects and solved tricky design problems in order to present, for example, time sequence, perspective, or three-dimensional structures.

An artist has a particular freedom in creating children's literature. The colorful work of Walter Crane and others combines fine design with practical lessons presented in an amusing way.

Children's pop-up books, which many of us had when growing up, are an old printer's tool used to surprise and charm the reader by breaking the surface of the page. Many early book designers were commissioned to develop ways of bringing goods, services, and ideas to the public. Architects and designers made pattern books to show everything from classical interiors of the ancient world to the latest in building plans. Stencil printing (*pochoir*), chromolithography, photography, woodcuts, and engravings are among the media refined and employed to display art in books effectively. Scrolls, adopted from Eastern cultures, gave artists freedom from a defined page and enabled them to present events sequentially.

Smithsonian researchers study pictorial sources in the collections to trace the origins of taste and attitudes toward decoration. Illustrated books often serve as the only remaining record of earlier works of art, buildings, gardens, and events. The journey of discovery represented by a book is, for cultural historians, a vital sign of the artistic mind. Social and cultural historians may gain ideas of daily life and values from illustrations. Trade literature represents the development of American manufacturing and marketing. Trade catalogs document the material aspirations of the rising middle class. Ephemeral pieces show how people designed and decorated their houses; what they ate, wore, and owned; and what they produced at work. For an exhibit specialist, design and trade literature can provide vital details for repair and display of museum objects and the decoration of period rooms.

Detail from MARK ATTWOOD, JOACHIM SCHÖNFELDT, AND ROBERT WEINEK, EDITORS, *GIF 2*, 1994.

Book Arts

HUMPHRY REPTON (1752–1818)
Observations on the Theory and Practice of Landscape Gardening. London: printed by T. Bensley for J. Taylor, 1803.

Essentially a trade catalog to show prospective clients how Repton could transform their grounds, *Observations* embodies his theories about creating formal landscapes for English country estates. Although Repton often incorporated neoclassical structures into his designs, they still retained a natural feel because of his strategic placement of loosely gathered-together trees and plants throughout. In this work, he supplied "Before" and "After" views of particular designs; the viewer lifts a paper flap to see the dramatically transformed garden.

WILLIAM MULLINGAR HIGGINS (ACT. 1830S)
The House Painter, or, Decorator's Companion: being a complete treatise on the origin of colour, the law of harmonious colouring, the manufacture of pigments, oils, and varnishes: and the art of house painting, graining, and marbling. London: Thomas Kelly, 1841. From the collection of Robert D. Mussey Jr.

One of many technical works on nineteenth-century craftsmanship in the collections of the Smithsonian Institution Libraries, this volume contains hand-painted illustrations of various wood grains along with instructions on how to achieve each effect. It was written for craftsmen, architects, and interior designers, and the illustrations in this copy, with their spatters and stains, show how often it was referred to in the workshop.

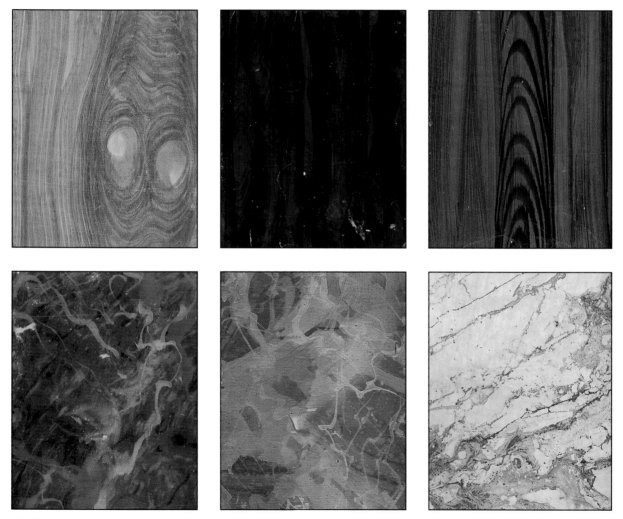

details

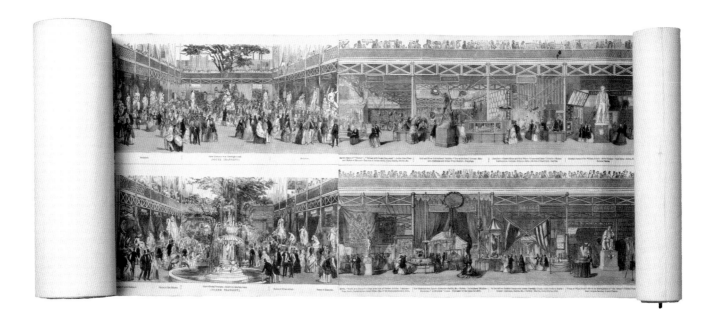

ILLUSTRATED LONDON NEWS
"Grand Panorama of the Great Exhibition of All
Nations." 1851. Friends of the Library Fund.

Created as a commemorative for the 1851 Great Exhibition held in London (commonly known as the
Crystal Palace exhibition), this 29-foot scroll depicts
the interior scenes and pavilions of the fair. Developed
by the staff of the *Illustrated London News,* the engraved
images convey the grandeur and expanse of this unique
historic event, which inspired the United States and
other European countries to mount their own international expositions.

HUBERT HOWE BANCROFT (1832–1918)
The Book of the Fair. Chicago and San Francisco, 1893.
Gift of Larry Zim World's Fair collection.

This standard history of the Chicago World's Columbian Exposition was presented as a limited edition to fair officials and sponsors. Supplemented with a hundred folio prints, among them signed etchings and photogravures, it is both a record of the fair and a fine example of chromolithography, or color printing. By displaying technological advances, industrial achievements, and popular entertainment, such publications document the worldview of a period.

WALTER CRANE (1845–1915)
A Romance of the Three Rs. London: Marcus Ward, 1886.
Mary Stuart Book Fund.

Walter Crane, a designer and illustrator of the British
Arts and Crafts movement, believed he could teach
children about good design by incorporating the latest
styles in his imaginative books for young people. He
eagerly promoted the publication of inexpensive soft-
cover picture books that a growing literate middle class
could afford. In *A Romance of the Three Rs,* which Crane
wrote for his young son Lionel, a boy experiences many
exciting adventures as he journeys around the world in
his quest to learn how to read and write.

FRANCES THEODORA PARSONS (1861–1952)
*According to Season: Talks about the Flowers in the Order
of Their Appearance in the Woods and Fields.* New York:
C. Scribner's Sons, 1894.

Frances Theodora Parsons started taking walks in the
countryside after the death of her first husband. These
strolls inspired her most popular book, *How to Know
the Wildflowers* (1893). *According to Season* is a collection
of the author's articles for the New York *Tribune.* This
special copy of the first edition contains nine original
watercolor sketches by an unknown artist.

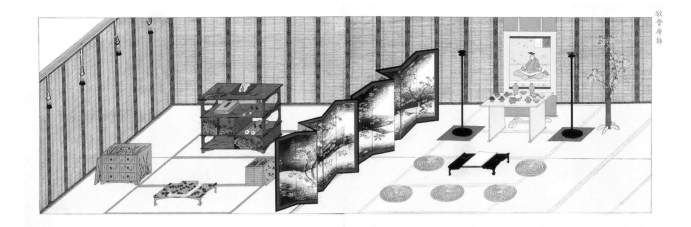

ASAMARO INOKUMA

Kyugi soshoku jurokushiki zufu (Sixteen pictorial charts of ancient ceremonial decoration). [Kyoto]: Kyoto Bijutsu Kyokai, 1903. Lillian Saxe Fund.

Produced as a commemorative for members of the Kyoto Art Society, this book presents sixteen Japanese interiors that contain implements required for the performance of sixteen traditional activities, including a poetry contest, a coming-of-age ritual, and a green-tea (*sencha*) gathering. Filled with distinctive Japanese patterns and details, the hand-colored woodblock illustrations depict decorative lacquered pieces, costumes, and furnishings. An extraordinarily beautiful object in its own right, the book provides a fascinating look at Japanese culture.

146

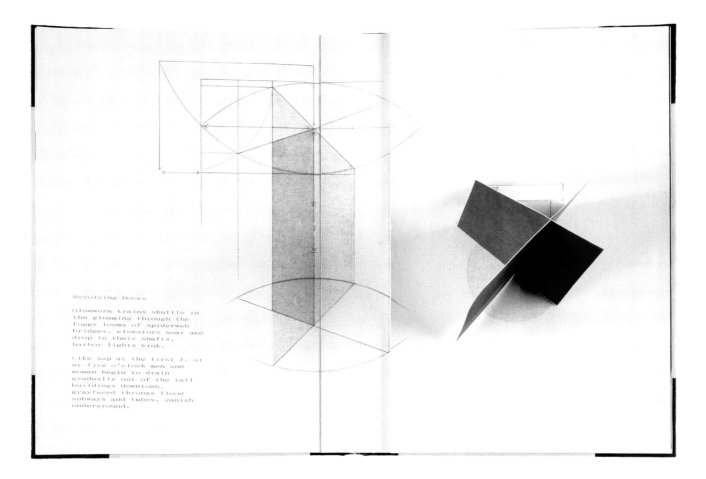

Revolving Doors

Glowworm trains shuttle in
the gloaming through the
foggy looms of spiderweb
bridges, elevators soar and
drop in their shafts,
harbor lights wink.

Like sap at the first frost
at five o'clock men and
women begin to drain
gradually out of the tall
buildings downtown,
grayfaced throngs flood
subways and tubes, vanish
underground.

SJOERD HOFSTRA (B. 1952)
They Pair Off Hurriedly. Amsterdam and New York:
ZET, 1992. Friends of the Library Fund.

In this remarkable book, Dutch-born artist Sjoerd
Hofstra showed himself to be a master of paper construction by creating highly dramatic pop-ups, including a revolving door and a cascade of rooftops. The
book is a reinterpretation of *Manhattan Transfer,* John
Dos Passos's 1925 novel, which captured the hustle and
bustle of daily life in New York City. Hofstra incorporated Dos Passos's text within printed pages that
resemble architectural drawings, so that the viewer
feels as if he or she is reading a blueprint.

Mark Attwood (b. 1966),
Joachim Schönfeldt (b. 1958),
and Robert Weinek (b. 1964), editors
GIF 2. Johannesburg: The Artists' Press in
collaboration with FIG Gallery, 1994.

GIF 2 consists of mounted prints, mixed media, photocopies, and a photograph in brown paper covers; it is
contained in a wooden slipcase with bronze animal
hooves attached to the front and back. The editors
compiled contemporary African artwork, signed and
numbered by eighteen artists, including Tamar Mason's
piece, shown above. It is housed in the National Museum of African Art Library, one of the most comprehensive reference collections in the world dealing with
African art and artists.

COEX'AE QGAM (B. 1935?)
*Qauqaua: A San Folk Story from Botswana Told by
Coex'ae Qgam.* Johannesburg: The Artists' Press, [1996].
S. Dillon Ripley Library Endowment.

Published in collaboration with the Kuru Art Project,
Qauqaua is a rendition of a folktale of the Naro people
of Botswana and the first book to be published in Naro
and English. Part of the folklore of Botswana, the
story is mythically connected to rock engravings that
are said to be the footprints of Qauqaua. Like earlier
exploration narratives, the book combines an artist's
object with the telling of a tale. It was hand-printed
in a limited edition of one hundred plus twenty artists'
proofs; the Smithsonian Libraries' copy is numbered
fifty-two.

Architecture and Design

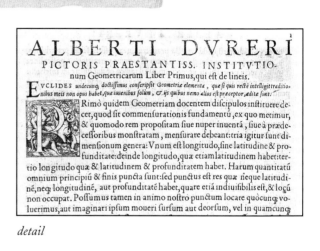

detail

Dürer, the famous German artist, was intensely interested in mathematics and its relation to art theory. In 1525 he published his work on the basic mathematics he felt an artist should know, including the construction of curves, polygons, bird's-eye and profile elevations, and the Platonic solids. The Smithsonian Libraries' copy is the 1535 Latin translation. Dürer's theoretical work was widely studied for centuries.

HANS VREDEMAN DE VRIES (1527–CA. 1604)
Perspective. [The Hague]: Hendrik Hondius, 1615.
Mary Stuart Book Fund.

Vredeman de Vries, a Dutch painter and architect, wrote and illustrated what became one of the major guidebooks on perspective for designers, painters, and architects. Perspective had been a part of the education of such professionals since the Renaissance. The book includes a number of scenes and projections employing one-point and multipoint perspective. These were essential demonstrations for artists of the day, including the Dutch painter Jan Vermeer (1632–1675), who was said to have a copy in his library.

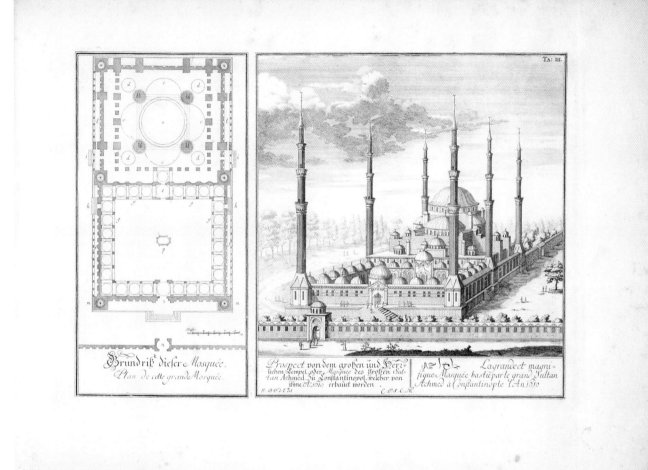

Brundriß dieser Mosquée.
Plan de cette grande Mosquée.

Prospect von dem großen und Herr=
lichen Tempel oder Mosquée des großen Sul=
tan Achmed zu Constantinopel welcher von
ihme A: 1610 erbauet worden

La grande et magni=
fique Mosquée bastie par le grand Sultan
Achmed à Constantinople l'An 1610

JOHANN BERNHARD FISCHER VON ERLACH
(1656–1723)
Entwurff einer historischen Architectur (A plan of civil
and historical architecture). Leipzig: [s.n.], 1725.
Trustees' Fund.

Fischer, principal architect for the Austrian court, developed residences, theaters, and churches in a Baroque
style that soon found imitators throughout the Habs-
burg empire. In the *Entwurff* he attempted the first
comparative history of the world's major structures
from antiquity to the eighteenth century, including
plans and elevations from ancient Greece and Rome.
Fischer was among the earliest writers to describe
and illustrate non-Western structures from the Middle
and Far East, for which he used Nieuhof's travel guide
(see pp. 76, 77) as one source of information. Fischer's
overview of a number of ornamental styles inspired
design revivals in the late eighteenth and early nineteenth centuries.

Journeys of the Imagination

GIUSEPPE GALLI BIBIENA (1696–1757)
Architetture, e prospettive (Architecture, and
perspective). Augsburg: Andrea Pfeffel, 1740.
Gift of Abram S. Hewitt.

Galli Bibiena, an Italian designer, employed intricate
systems of perspective to create dramatic illusionary
theater sets and festival decorations for the royal
families of Austria and Germany. In *Architetture* he
documents the ostentatious styles of the period with
fifty engravings of altars, palace interiors, and theater
sets, many of them for religious festivals in Vienna.

Le garde meuble (The furniture repository). Paris, (1839–1935).

Published between 1839 and 1935, this highly influential serial helped to disseminate French design throughout Europe and America. Each issue of *Le garde meuble* contained nine plates illustrating the latest in interiors and furniture. Because of the quality of the plates, designers were able to replicate intricate details and patterns.

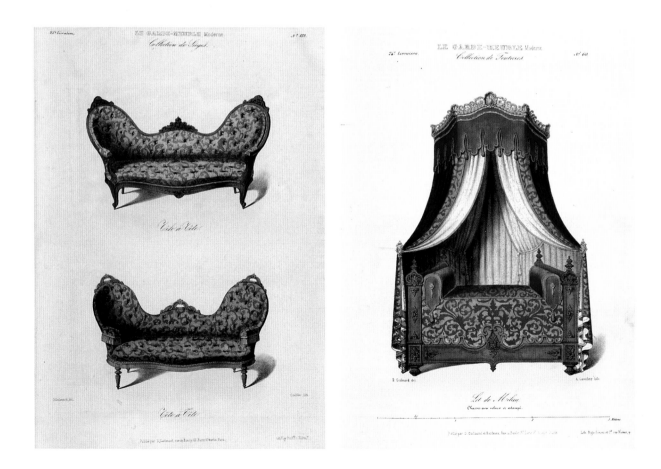

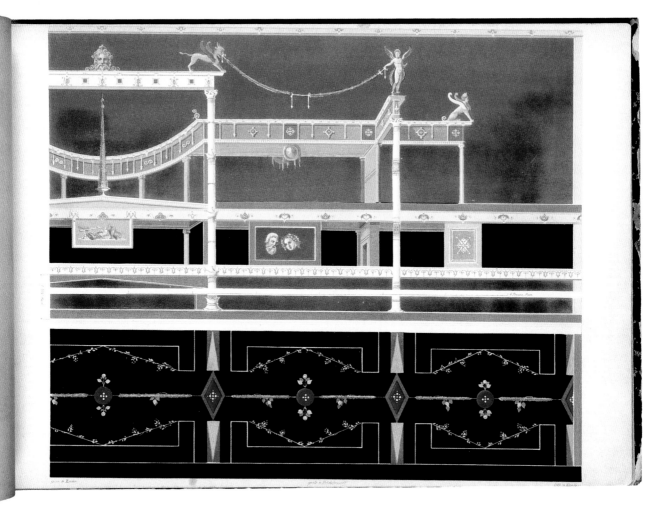

WILHELM ZAHN (1800–1871)
Ornamente aller klassischen Kunstepochen (Ornaments
of all classical periods in art). Berlin: G. Reimer, 1843.

Traveling in Italy in the 1820s, Zahn recorded ornamental patterns at Pompeii and Herculaneum, as
well as the interiors of the sixteenth-century Palazzo
Del Te in Mantua designed by Giuliano Romano.
He published *Ornamente,* with its copious examples
of classical, medieval, and Renaissance ornament,
to educate designers in the neoclassical and Renaissance styles.

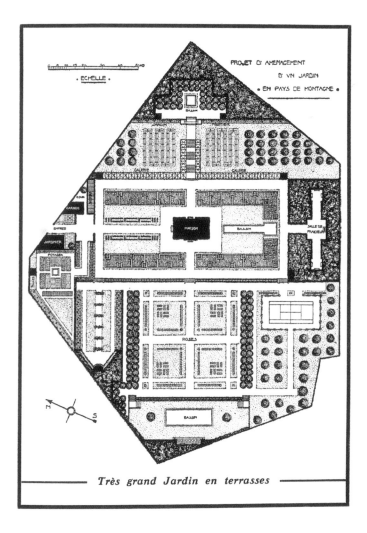

Très grand Jardin en terrasses

left

ANDRÉ VERA
Le nouveau jardin (The new garden). Paris: Émile-Paul Éditeur, [1912].

The brothers André and Paul Vera, designers in the Art Moderne style, here present their concepts for very formal gardens emphasizing clarity, harmony, distinctive proportions, and bold color. Their plans encompassed gardens of various sizes and purposes, such as a trellised garden and gardens for beekeeping and fruit cultivation. While their ideas were in direct contrast to the curvilinear Art Nouveau designs of the day, they were very much in keeping with some theories of Le Corbusier, the Machine Age architect who was then developing his formal aesthetic. However, the use of woodblock prints for the illustrations does give this book a handcrafted feel.

KARL BLOSSFELDT (1865–1932)
Urformen der Kunst (Art forms in nature). Berlin: E. Wasmuth, [1928?]. Pierpont Morgan Fund, 1942.

Around 1918 Blossfeldt used a microscopic lens to make detailed photographs of plant forms against a stark background. Stripped of their naturalistic quality, the plants appeared to be man-made cast-iron forms. The creation of this book coincided with the birth of the Bauhaus school of design, which emulated machinelike forms and rid objects of ornamentation that did not contribute to their function. Design schools adopted Blossfeldt's work as a pattern book for natural forms for many decades.

E. A. SÉGUY (ACT. 1900–1925)
Papillons (Butterflies). [Paris: Tolmer, ca. 1925].

This splendid example of a pattern book features some
twenty plates with two types of illustrations: realistic
depictions of butterflies and those in which butterflies
are transformed into abstract forms and ornamental
patterns. Séguy achieved the exceptional vibrancy and
color of these prints by using the *pochoir* process, a
method of silkscreen stenciling. Séguy intended the
book to be an inspiration for designers, especially those
specializing in wall coverings and textiles.

Journeys of the Imagination

Trade Literature

YOKOHAMA NURSERY CO., LTD.
Maples of Japan. Yokohama, Japan, 1898.

The Yokohama Nursery, with offices in New York and Japan, was one of the largest suppliers of Japanese plants and bulbs to the Western nursery trade. With *pochoir* stencil illustrations effectively presenting the vivid colors of leaves, the Yokohama export catalogs created much of the early interest in Japanese maples in the United States. The Smithsonian Libraries Horticulture collection, strong in nineteenth-century landscape design and garden practice, is augmented by garden furniture and other items related to the florist trade. Smithsonian horticulturists maintain period gardens and complementary plantings around every museum.

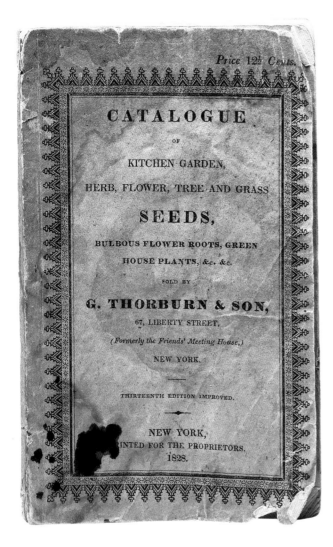

G. THORBURN AND SON

Catalogue of Kitchen Garden, Herb, Flower, Tree and Grass Seeds . . . 13th ed. New York, 1828.

Grant Thorburn, born in Scotland in 1773, arrived in New York in 1794 at age twenty-one. He was a nail-maker and sold novelties and hardware in the city, but when he found that his best sales were for flowers in pots, he turned to the seed business. His was probably the first American business of importance to sell stock seeds. The 1822 Thorburn catalog was the first seed book in America to be issued in pamphlet form and the first to include illustrations.

WILLIAM PRINCE
Catalogue of Fruit and Ornamental Trees and Plants,
Bulbous Flower Roots, Green-house Plants, . . .
Long Island, N.Y., 1823.

The Prince garden on Long Island was the first major
commercial nursery in the United States. It became
the largest and most important American nursery of
the eighteenth and early nineteenth centuries. Its first
known advertisement is dated September 21, 1767, and
its earliest catalog was published as a broadside in 1771.
Many of the shrubs and flowers collected from the
Lewis and Clark expedition were sent to the Prince
nursery for propagation and distribution. The nursery
also trained most of the early plantsmen in the United
States.

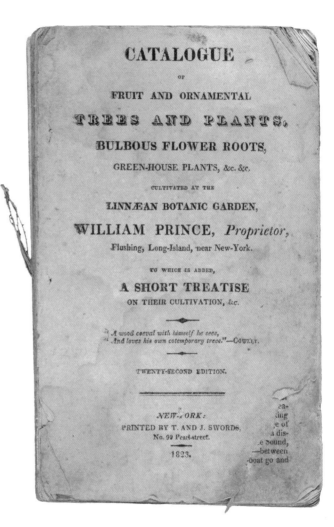

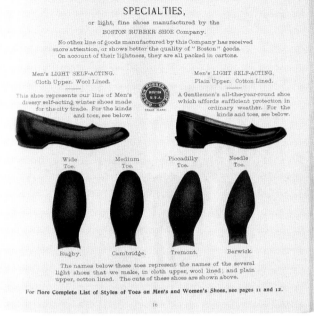

BOSTON RUBBER SHOE COMPANY
[Catalog]. Boston, [1895?].

Chromolithography, a color printing technique of
the mid to late 1800s, often resembles oil painting or
watercolor. This catalog of the Boston Rubber Shoe
Company used chromolithographs to great effect. To
illustrate the variety and appropriateness of its boots
for different outdoorsmen, the Boston Rubber Shoe
Company depicted them on fishermen, hunters, and
loggers. In another approach, similar to today's life-
style advertising, the company also pictured proper
Bostonians on rainy days set against famous city land-
marks, including the Boston Public Library.

right

WILLIAM DOXFORD AND SONS, LTD.
"Doxford Opposed Piston Oil Engine." Sunderland,
England, 1922.

The shipbuilding and marine engineering firm of
William Doxford and Sons developed the opposed-
piston marine oil engine. To illustrate its unusual
operation, the firm devised this paper-and-board
model with movable pistons and levers.

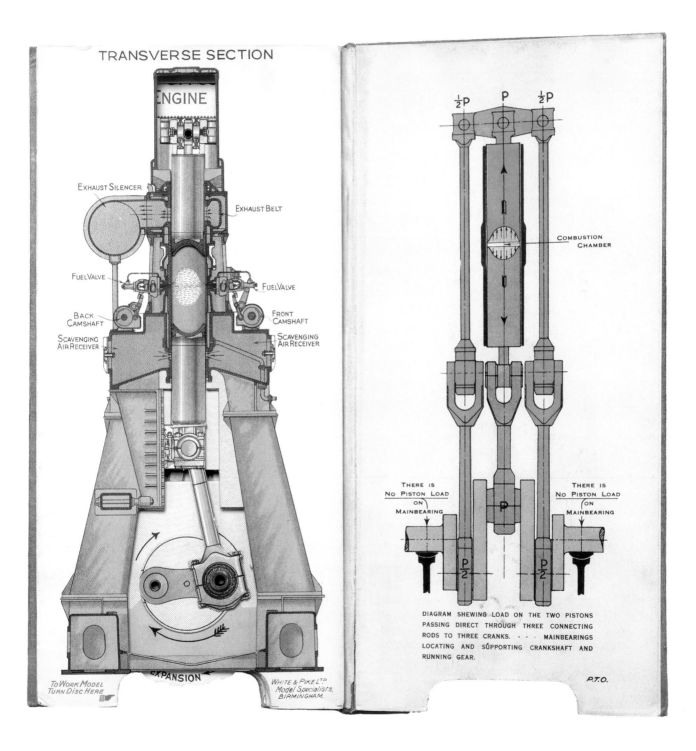

TRANSVERSE SECTION

ENGINE

Exhaust Silencer

Exhaust Belt

Fuel Valve

Fuel Valve

Back Camshaft

Front Camshaft

Scavenging Air Receiver

Scavenging Air Receiver

EXPANSION

To Work Model Turn Disc Here

White & Pike Ltd. Model Specialists, Birmingham.

½P   P   ½P

Combustion Chamber

There is No Piston Load on Mainbearing

There is No Piston Load on Mainbearing

P

P/2   P/2

DIAGRAM SHEWING LOAD ON THE TWO PISTONS PASSING DIRECT THROUGH THREE CONNECTING RODS TO THREE CRANKS. · · · MAINBEARINGS LOCATING AND SUPPORTING CRANKSHAFT AND RUNNING GEAR.

P.T.O.

SEARS, ROEBUCK AND CO.
"Brick Veneer 'Honor Bilt' Homes."
[Chicago], 1930.

During a fifteen-year period, Sears shipped the components for 49,500 "kit-houses," providing middle-class
Americans with good residential design at affordable
prices. Buyers selected their dream houses from the
scores of models presented in Sears's "Honor Bilt"
catalogs. For historians, details of house design, such
as the kitchen breakfast nook, and slogans, such as
"Where women spend $2/3$ of every day should be modern and bright," are important records of American
domestic life.

left

UNITED STEEL COMPANIES, LTD.
[Lacquer strips]. February 1933.

right

LUCIUS AND BRUNING
Dye lot samples. [n.d.].

SPENCERIAN STEEL PEN COMPANY
Pen nibs. [New York, 1937?].

One of the most direct marketing methods is to show
a product in a memorable or eye-catching manner to
clients. Clever designers devised ways to incorporate
samples into product literature. These examples include
colorful lacquer strips, brightly tinted threads indicating dye lots, and pen points and their corresponding
signature styles.

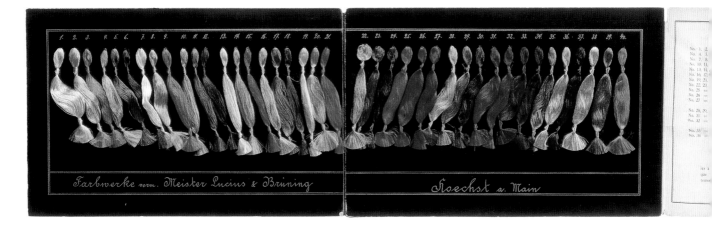

Farbwerke vorm. Meister Lucius & Brüning — *Hoechst a. Main*

Index

Facsimile of a preconquest codex, probably from the Mixteca, which covers calendrical, astonomical, and mythological subjects. One of the five divinatory screenfolds of the Borgia group. These scarce fragments constitute a principal resource for study of Precolumbian cultures of the Americas. *Codex Cospianus.* Rome, 1989.

Note: Illustrations are indicated by page numbers in *italics.*

Acknowledgments

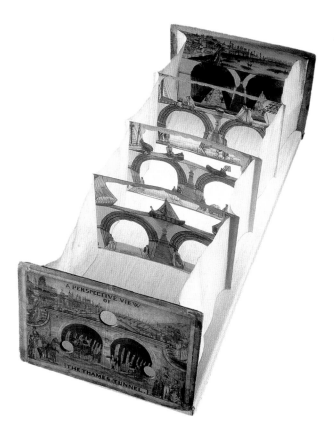

Souvenir peep-show book published for visitors to the construction site of the first modern submarine tunnel under the Thames River. Many German, French, and British tourists came to witness this marvel of invention. *Perspectivische Ansicht des Tunnels unter der Themse* [Perspective View of the Tunnel under the Thames]. London, ca. 1825.

*M*any people were involved in producing *An Odyssey in Print* and its catalog, the publication before you. It is my honor to acknowledge them. Our hope is that, through text and display, audiences will learn about the rich collections the Smithsonian Libraries preserves as part of our national heritage.

Smithsonian Institution Libraries Director Nancy E. Gwinn had the original vision for a traveling exhibition of treasures from our collections. Nancy has given her unwavering support to making the Smithsonian Libraries better known through this exhibition, contributing both her extensive knowledge of Smithsonian history and her tireless fund-raising skills. Rare Book Curators Ronald Brashear, Leslie Overstreet, Paul McCutcheon, and Stephen Van Dyk deserve special mention for selecting fascinating and well-loved items from their collections and writing compellingly to argue their inclusion. Librarians Angela Haggins, Alvin Hutchinson, Rhoda S. Ratner, Marca Woodhams, and Janet Stanley suggested titles from the general collection that illustrated the theme of how people use books at the Smithsonian.

It was a privilege to work with two talented guest essayists. Michael Dirda of the *Washington*

Post cheerfully took on the task of inspiring readers with a piece on the enduring value of books. Storrs L. Olson provided a crucial explanation of the value of books within the Institution and described the important interaction between librarians and scholars. Smithsonian Libraries Public Information Officer Nancy L. Matthews and her assistant Savannah Schroll contributed a great deal of time and expertise in producing this book. Their careful editing and organizing of the images strengthened the presentation of the history and collections of the Smithsonian Libraries. Laudine Creighton provided budgetary oversight and mastered the complexities of new and different contract procedures to assure a fine result. Volunteers Jennifer Engelbach and Lee Taylor Chan created a database of collections information from Smithsonian Institution annual reports that gave fascinating glimpses of the Libraries' growth. I wish to acknowledge a debt to my colleague, the late Ellen B. Wells, a former rare books librarian at the Libraries. Ellen's love for the breadth and variety of special collections manifested itself in the encyclopedic knowledge she conveyed to her associates.

The elegant book before you is a consequence of the Libraries' association with Ed Marquand and designer Susan Kelly of Marquand Books and with editor Suzanne Kotz. With their expertise and assistance, the Smithsonian Libraries have a work of permanent value.

In New York City, Eric J. Holzenberg, Librarian and Director of the Grolier Club, helped to shape the exhibition and the related programs. Grolier Club President William Buice and Exhibitions Committee chair Peter Kraus have been enthusiastic throughout, offering thoughtful advice. Nancy Houghton, Registrar for the Grolier Club, has been a dedicated liaison, providing enormous support and encouragement in addition to helpful contacts for publicity.

Susan R. Frampton, Preservation Services, and William E. Baxter and Bonnie Sousa of the Dibner Library of the History of Science and Technology contributed considerable time to planning, organizing, and executing thousands of details involved in bringing an exhibition to life. The Libraries' Book Conservation Laboratory staff Claire Dekle, Leslie Long, John Glavan, and volunteer Jahanvi Desai ensured that each book was prepared for safe travel and display, to be returned undamaged for the use of future readers. Janice Stagnitto Ellis, a former Libraries staff member, provided skilled restoration and was instrumental in the installation of the exhibition. David Holbert promptly supplied digital images throughout the process. Martin Kalfatovic created the web version of the exhibition at www.sil.si.edu. Gwen Leighty, Development Officer, and Dale Miller, Development Associate, not only raised funds but also created public events to heighten the educational component of the exhibition. Hilary Hoopes served as educational consultant to this project and helped the Smithsonian Libraries reach out to wider audiences.

The Smithsonian Office of Exhibits Central supported the exhibition in many ways. Lynn Kawaratani's designs realized the "journey" theme in a lively exhibition at the Grolier Club, and Eve McIntyre elegantly recast the exhibition for Washington, D.C. Ann Carper thoughtfully edited and enhanced exhibition text, and Rolando Mayan produced and installed many of the graceful details in New York City; Paula Kaufman ably managed the myriad issues of installation in Washington,

D.C. The Smithsonian Office of Imaging, Printing, and Photographic Services extended themselves to provide images on demand.

John Tsantes is the photographer of most of the images in this book. His fine skills and good eye help immeasurably to bring to life the amazing variety of volumes in the Smithsonian Libraries collections. Other photographs appearing in this work were done by staff of the Smithsonian Office of Imaging, Printing, and Photographic Services and by Jon Goell and Matt Flynn. We thank them all.

My contributions to this book and to the exhibition could not have been completed without the love and understanding of, and the errands run by, George D. Thomas. My thanks to him and to the many Smithsonian staff who work to keep the national collections for future generations.

MARY AUGUSTA THOMAS